Dog Doing Well

Stories from My Life in the Soviet Union

Sonya Vesterholt

Translated by Nina Sokol

CHERRY ORCHARD BOOKS

2025

Library of Congress Cataloging-in-Publication Data

Names: Vesterholt, Sonja, 1945- author | Sokol, Nina translator
Title: Dog doing well : stories from my life in the Soviet Union / Sonya Vesterholt ; translated by Nina Sokol.
Other titles: Hunden er rask.. English
Description: Boston : Cherry Orchard Books, 2025. | Translation of: Hunden er rask
Identifiers: LCCN 2025018103 (print) | LCCN 2025018104 (ebook) | ISBN 9798887198279 hardback | ISBN 9798887198286 paperback | ISBN 9798887198293 adobe pdf | ISBN 9798887198309 epub
Subjects: LCSH: Vesterholt, Sonja, 1945---Childhood and youth | Soviet Union. Komitet gosudarstvennoĭ bezopasnosti | Saint Petersburg (Russia)--Biography | LCGFT: Biographies
Classification: LCC HQ637 .V47513 2025 (print) | LCC HQ637 (ebook)
LC record available at https://lccn.loc.gov/2025018103
LC ebook record available at https://lccn.loc.gov/2025018104

Copyright © English Translation, Academic Studies Press, 2025.
Published in Danish by Gyldendal in 2011.
ISBN 9798887198279 (hardback)
ISBN 9798887198286 (paperback)
ISBN 9798887198293 (adobe pdf)
ISBN 9798887198309 (epub)

Book design by Lapiz Digital Services.
Cover design by Ivan Grave.
Illustrations on the cover and on p. 8 by Alexander Florensky, reproduced by permission.

Published by Cherry Orchard Books, an imprint of Academic Studies Press.
1007 Chestnut Street
Newton, MA 02464
press@academicstudiespress.com
www.academicstudiespress.com

This book was published with the generous support of the Danish Arts Foundation.

For Anna

The author thanks Ilya Katsnelson for his invaluable help in the preparation of the English edition of this book.

When I was writing this book, I thought that the monster has crawled back into its lair to lick its wounds.
But *now it is everywhere!*

Contents

How the Steel Was Tempered	9
The Day of the Cat	22
Dog Doing Well	36
Lolita Torres	39
"Shitty Couch" on the Wings of History	58
Sex in the Soviet Union	67
Alyosha	81
Kaliningrad	95
The Scent of the Taiga	104
Sausages with Stewed Cabbage	115
Roadside Picnic	126
The Last Summer	137
A Happy Death	148
My Father	158
Transit to Paradise	186
About the Author	193

In collaboration with Britta Sørensen

How the Steel Was Tempered

On board a spaceship there lurks an indescribably horrible, slimy, and dangerous creature, a killer, that attacks the crew. One by one. The creature is not visible, which is what makes the fear it evokes all the more pronounced. *Alien* is the most terrifying film I have ever seen in my whole life. At the very end, when a courageous woman finally manages to defeat the creature on her own, you see it disappear in a short glimpse out into space to the tones of triumphant music. At which point the creature suddenly strikes one as being rather ridiculous and not in the least bit terrifying. It resembles a seahorse more than anything else. I understand perfectly well why the creator of the film chose to show the creature in those short glimpses. It is impossible to imagine the sheer horror one feels at the thought of such a slimy, invisible thing. That was how I felt about the KGB who tried to enlist me as their spy back when I married a Dane and was waiting for my permit to travel to Denmark. The KGB, Komitet Gosudarstvennoy Bezopasnosti, Committee for State Security, foreign intelligence and domestic security agency of the Soviet Union, the slimy monster that thrived below the surface of the Soviet Union and continues to live to this very day, just under a different name...

After I had lived in Denmark for many years, I decided to take my daughter for a visit to the Soviet Union under glasnost and perestroika. Anna, who was born and raised in Copenhagen, was fifteen at the time. The morning after our arrival the telephone in our hotel room rang. A man's voice asked to speak with Sofia Lazarevna.

> In Russia, when approaching someone officially, you address them by their first name and their patronymic (based on their father's first name). Take my name for example. In my passport, it says my name is Sofia. My friends call me Sonya, Sofa, or Sonyechka. They are all one and the same name. My father's name was Lazar. That's why, when I was living in the Soviet Union, the name in my passport was: Sofia Lazarevna.
>
> Example 1: Ivan Vladimirovich Ivanov is the son of Vladimir. Their surnames are Ivanov. The son is mostly referred to as Vanya by his friends (Remember *Uncle Vanya*?) Or Vanyechka.
>
> Example 2: Maria Alexandrovna Ivanova is the daughter of Alexander. Her surname is Ivanova. An "a" is added to her father's surname because she is a woman. Among friends she is known as Masha, Mashenka, etc.

That is precisely why Russia is insurmountable. There are too many people who have at least three different names. It's impossible for anyone other than the Russians to keep track of.

There is only one official office in the world that has ever referred to me as Sofia Lazarevna and that is the KGB. The voice said that the call was being made from the hotel reception desk. He asked me to come down because it seemed that there were a few problems with my passport, which I had handed into the reception the day before. I immediately felt the old sense of horror returning. It was "them." I woke up Anna and explained to her that she was to follow me and, if I at any point made a special signal to her, she was to take a taxi out to my friends and wait for me there. My poor daughter, why in the world had I dragged her here with me? She had only been to the Soviet Union once before and she had been one year old then. She was now fifteen and, thank goodness, knew nothing about these monstrosities. My sleepy child simply had no idea what I was talking about but obediently followed me.

Down in the reception Anna and I were escorted into a room where two men were sitting. I hadn't sat across from the KGB since the 1970s when I, for the umpteenth time, refused to cooperate with them. Whereupon I was refused permission to enter the Soviet Union for the next fourteen years. This was now the year 1989. It would still be two more years before the Soviet Union finally collapsed.

The men didn't mention a word about my passport. It was as though they picked up the thread from the 1970s, only now they made inquiries into my friends and colleagues in Denmark. I grew furious. What made them think that I wanted to speak to them now after I had refused to do it so many times in the past, after they had punished me with an entry ban? I hadn't even been allowed to come for my father's funeral. I shouted all those things to them. Whereupon one of the men said in an accusing tone to his colleague, "Can't you see that it's hopeless? She doesn't care for her motherland in the least!" I got to my feet. "And do you think you're my motherland?" I spluttered and marched out of the room with Anna at my heels. "What was that all about?" she asked, perplexed. Standing in a semi-dark hall in a Soviet hotel I began to explain everything to my Danish child about the Committee for State Security and about the slimy monster's function. "But they're spies!" Anna exclaimed. I began to laugh hysterically. That was the last time that the monster had shown its face to me.

It all began twenty years earlier. An early morning in 1970. I had just married a Dane, Ole Vesterholt. And what is a newly married couple typically preoccupied with early in the morning if they're not sleeping? Exactly what one imagines. In the middle of our lovemaking, the telephone rang. I reached for the receiver, hoping it would be a short call. A man's voice on the other end said: "Sofia Lazarevna?" He explained that he was calling from the university dorm where my husband really should have been residing because foreign students weren't allowed to live privately with anyone. But Ole had moved in with me ten days after we had met and had continued living with me for nine months already. The voice said that since Ole wasn't occupying his living quarters at the dorm there were certain things that had to be straightened out, so he was calling to ask Ole to come to the dorm immediately. I hung up the phone and turned to Ole: "It's them," I said and could distinctively feel the monster breathing down my neck. "Let's go there together right away."

When we got there, no one there knew anything about a phone call. Ole decided to look in on one of his classmates while I waited for him downstairs. The moment he disappeared up the stairs two men entered the building and grabbed hold of me, saying, "Follow us." They did not bother identifying themselves nor did they say why I was to follow them. They assumed that all Soviet citizens automatically knew who they were and where they came from. They escorted me into their waiting car and we drove around the block and stopped. There were very few foreigners in the Soviet Union at that time, and Ole and I were perfectly aware that someone was keeping an eye on us and that our telephones were being bugged. Nevertheless, this was the very first time that I actually saw the monster's exposed face.

What happens to a person when they are confronted with the ultimate horror? The all-powerful authoritarian KGB provoked the ultimate sense of fear and terror in the consciousness of all Soviet citizens. The monster always lay in wait, lurking just below the surface. What would they do to me now? Devour me? Shoot me? Torture me?

None of the above. Instead, they began almost apologetically to explain that they had merely wanted to have a little talk with me. They had tried to lure Ole to his dorm assuming that I would have stayed at home. In that way they could have spoken to me undisturbed. But we had both gone. They now ordered me to go back to Ole and say that I had just met a friend who needed me to help her with something. He wasn't to know that I had fallen into the clutches of the KGB. He was just to go home. I got out of the car, walked around the corner and entered the dorm where Ole was already looking for me. I said in a very loud voice that I had just met a friend with whom I needed to talk. Then, with my lips, I mouthed the letters K-G-B, because I wasn't sure what the KGB was capable of. Perhaps they had put a bug on me without my knowing it. Ole was easily able to read my lips and turned deathly pale. I left the building again, turned the corner, and got into the KGB car, and we drove off.

Thankfully, very few people in our peaceful part of the world truly know how they would react when confronted with an extreme situation; however, you don't know your true self if you've never faced an ultimate threat of any kind in your life. You don't know yourself if you have never been exposed to being in the dilemma of having to choose between being a traitor, an informer, or some other detestable thing. That is the dilemma you are forced to face when encountering the KGB.

The car drove through my wonderful city, Leningrad, across two bridges and past the pink-colored palaces. The city was full of life. People. It was springtime. And I was thinking... no, I can't claim to know what I was thinking on that day nearly fifty years ago, but what I did know back then was who I was. In the repressive society which the Soviet Union was at that time, it was easy to frighten and break us all. We all lived in a kind of swamp-like condition covered by a dry surface of bodies that had been annihilated with time. It was the ones who were strong, the courageous ones, the ones who were different and the stray ones that had turned into a vulnerable crust.

They say that St. Petersburg is built on human bones. The fact is that, at the start of the eighteenth century, the then Russian tsar, Peter the Great, decided to build a new capital. He wanted to transform Russia and open the window to the West. Hundreds of thousands of serfs were called in from all over Russia to build the city, and they died like flies in the process, becoming mere building material as a result. Two hundred years later, society was to undergo a major transformation once again. Nineteen seventeen became the decisive year. With the revolution, the "window to the West" was hermetically sealed and the Soviet Union was built. Again on human bones. Why was it that every time something new was to be built in Russia it was always on human bones?

That which at that time was referred to as the KGB was responsible for the destruction. Now the slimy monster was dragging me through the city through its vile stomach. I wasn't going to allow it to digest me that easily. I already had some experience in dealing with it. I was only eleven years old when I stood face to face with myself for the first time and was forced to make a decision.

On an old class photo I am sitting next to a white-haired lady with dimples and wearing a white lace collar. Our classroom teacher. Distinguished-looking, with her hair pulled back and done up in a small bun. She was my first teacher and an important figure in the first four years of my schooling. Who among us can't claim to harbor tender feelings for our first teacher? However, the only thing I can recall about this woman is that she made me into a traitor. That might sound like I managed in my early school years to reveal classified information behind the atom bomb, but I hadn't. It was much worse than that. We grew up on movies and literature about the Civil War and the Great Patriotic War—what is known in the West as the Second World War—with stories about heroic partisans that, despite being subject to the most horrendous torture, never gave away the secrets to the enemy. We were brought up to sacrifice ourselves for our country. We were to inform against and betray one another in the name of our country. The Soviet Union was more important than anything else. If your friend had done something wrong, you were considered to be a bad friend if you didn't help him do the right thing. You were a bad friend if you didn't inform on your friend.

Every day we were reminded of our patriotic duty. In the classroom there hung a picture of a boy wearing a white shirt and a red scarf around his neck. Defiant and proud, his arms stretched out, he stands before three male family members. The boy was our hero, our saint, our ideal. Pavlik Morozov was his name. After the revolution, when the country lay in ruins and was unable to feed its own citizens, its agricultural industry having been demolished, and its people were starving, special military units were sent throughout the countryside to claim grain from the farmers and send it to the cities. Pavlik's father had hidden a bag of wheat in order to feed his hungry family, but the young loyal pioneer, Pavlik, informed on his father. At least, that is what we were told. There are several different versions with regard to what the father had done wrong. Some of them had been given the state- authorized stamp of approval, others were heretical.

1. He had hidden bread intended for his family.
2. He had helped some people who were being pursued by the government.
3. He had been a violent drunkard.
4. He had left Pavlik's mother for another woman.

The nature of his crime doesn't really matter. The point of the whole story was that Pavlik had turned his father in. There was no doubt as to where one's responsibility lay: one was first and foremost a pioneer, and then, and only then, a son. One's responsibility to one's country was greater than to one's family. All Soviet children knew the story about Pavlik, and the picture in the classroom was our daily reminder of it. The authorities picked up the grain and the father was deported and later executed. Subsequently, Pavlik's grandfather and his cousin slaughtered both Pavlik and his little brother, who unfortunately happened to be taking a walk with Pavlik in the forest when the execution was to take place. Whereupon, the state killed the rest of the family. It was all those massacres that hung on the wall of our classroom.

But back to my personal path to Golgotha. Everyone knows the classic story about the note that is secretly circulated hand-to-hand around the classroom until it finally ends up in the hands of the teacher. That was exactly what happened to me. I was in the fourth grade, and the year before our girls school had turned co-ed. Boy meets girl, but we girls were still brought up to have Victorian virtues and it was shameful to have anything to do with the boys besides those things of a scholastic nature. Then the day came when one of the boys in the school had written a note to my girlfriend, and suddenly the teacher was standing there waving it in the air. She meticulously chose me, the good friend. After school was let out, the teacher led me across the street and to a small park across from the school.

I had never before been alone with her and thought the whole thing to be rather strange. What did she intend to do with me? Why had we left the school grounds? She led me over to a bench, where we sat down in the sun. It became apparent that the time had now come where I was to fulfill my obligation and thereby become a worthy member of society. In other words, become an informer. With all the partisans in mind, I refused to reveal the name of the instigator. Whereupon, she gave a small lecture about destructive elements in the class, in society, in life, in the entire country. Suddenly, the fate of the entire country lay on my shoulders. She appealed to my conscience and my sense of duty. But that didn't work either. Right before my very eyes, this nice-looking and noble woman transformed into the slimy monster, which I would be able to recognize for the rest of my life anywhere, anytime.

But I had a weak point: my mother, who was already seriously ill at the time. The teacher knew that. She threatened that, if I didn't deliver the sinner's name, she would immediately go home to my mother and tell her what a big criminal I was. And that would most certainly be damaging to my mother for the rest of her life—she might even die from it, the teacher emphasized. Like many other partisans that were able to endure unimaginable pain under torture but broke if you threatened to torture one of their family members, I too, broke. I gave her the name of the boy.

Whereupon, the monster immediately transformed back into a nice old lady. She praised me, got up, and left. I howled at the top of my lungs and was on the verge of drowning in my own tears, as I rushed to the boy's house to warn him. He wasn't at home. So I searched for him everywhere and found the sinner playing soccer with some of the other boys. I confessed my crime to him, and he received my tear-sodden repentance with a stoic calm. He didn't care.

Since then I have always been able to sympathize with the pain felt by a traitor.

Knock-knock. *Stuk-stuk*. Who's there? In order for a system like the KGB's to survive, millions of compliant citizens have to be indoctrinated. We were to become *stukach*, from the Russian word *stuk*: to knock on the door; in other words, to be the one knocking on the door of the KGB, an informer. Through three generations, *stukach* was one of the most important words in the Russian language. It was a person like any other with two ears and two legs, but that person always harbored a secret inside. How did you make a person become a *stukach*? Some did it voluntarily in order to gain access to certain benefits, others were forced to do it. The whole of society was subject to informers. *Stuk-stuk*.

Why was everyone so afraid of telling others about their connection to the KGB? Why were they so afraid to reveal that the KGB had attempted to get them to tell something... about someone... about something or other? Imagine if everyone had shouted in the streets and at their workplaces, "The KGB has tried to recruit me but I refuse to have anything to do with them." Why were people so afraid of saying that? I'll tell you why. If you agreed to cooperate with the KGB, you would merely risk getting sticky with its slippery smile, but if you refused to cooperate with them, you risked ruining the rest of your life. The power elite controlled the society with the help of the KGB, and the KGB knew everything about you.

Most people have a soft spot in their lives, which can be used to manipulate them. If you were studying at the university, you risked getting kicked out if you refused to cooperate. If you had a job, you risked being stopped in your career path. If you were so courageous as to risk everything in the name of integrity, they could always threaten to hurt your loved ones. I was fortunate enough to experience the pain of being an informer relatively early in my life. This experience vaccinated me against treachery.

There were a few times during the course of the Soviet Union's existence where the monster received a slap in the face. In 1956—three years after Stalin's death—a Party congress was held where people talked openly for the first time about the monster's bloody victims, about the Gulag camps, and about the millions of murdered people. It was attributed to a single person, Stalin, and his forty-year reign of terror and murders. The man in question was dead anyway, so it was very convenient. The system remained infallible. Back then, Stalin's statues and portraits were removed. Many prisoners returned from the camps. They were rehabilitated and declared innocent to society. In many cases after their death.

I grew up during the "thaw," back when you talked openly about the crimes of the earlier times. My classmates and I were twelve years old at the time. Precisely the age when you start thinking in grander terms. Once again, I was fortunate because we lived in a time when we began to grasp that nothing lasts forever and that things change. One day I could be passing by a statue of Stalin, and the next day it might be gone. One day I could be passing by the portraits of him and Lenin hanging together on the walls of our classroom, the next day a bare spot might be visible next to a picture of a towering Lenin. Statues and portraits were removed during the night.

One morning, on the square next to the Baltiysky Station there stood a crane in front of the majestic statue of Stalin. I had spent the night at my aunt's who lived nearby and had to get up at the crack of dawn to get to school on time. The streets were deserted, and I stood outside the train station waiting for the bus that would take me to the other end of town. Without any great to-do, the crane placed its noose around the neck of the statue and removed Stalin.

What then? Yes, what then? It was necessary to promise the bewildered population something or other, so they were assured that communism would occur twenty years from then. Otherwise, what was all the hunger and terrorism for? Up until then, communism had been a phenomenon situated somewhere or other, at some point or other in the future, like a paradise everyone was waiting to enter. A deadline for it had now been fixed.

Communism took the place of the old religion. It had its very own new testament and its own saints. The new testament was Nikolai Ostrovsky's book *How the Steel Was Tempered*, from which all Soviet children were to memorize a particular passage:

> The most precious thing a person has is life. It is given to him only once and he must live it in such a way that, in looking back, he will not regret for years lived pointlessly and will not feel ashamed for a petty and worthless past— so that while dying he will be able to say, "I have devoted my whole life and strength to the most splendid cause in the world—the struggle for the liberation of mankind."

You have to start small, so I started with myself.

Now, many years later, in 1970, I had married a foreigner and was applying for an exit permit, which I couldn't obtain unless I gave something in exchange for it. Quid pro quo. The years had passed, but the monster still existed. In contrast to the Loch Ness monster, there was no doubt that this monster existed. It could be struck, and, while it was weak and collecting itself for a brief period, I grew up big and strong. Whereupon it began swishing its tail once again.

> —What is the tallest building in Leningrad? The KGB's building, because you can see Siberia from its basement.

I was anxious to see whether they would drive me to the KGB headquarters, but we drove down the main street, Nevsky Prospekt, and past the Moskovsky train station. The monster had secret rooms all over Leningrad. We arrived at a completely different building. The sign said it was the local office of the Communist Party. Of course! The monster hid behind the facade of the Party. They escorted me past the security guard, down a long hallway, to what appeared to be a dead end. Or so I thought, but, in reality, there was an invisible door hidden in the wall. I was escorted into the monster's cave, which turned out to be a perfectly ordinary office space. "Have a seat," one of the KGB officers said and added, "Your mother is seriously ill, isn't that right?"

The Day of the Cat

My mother once ate a cat. All my life I have tried to imagine various scenarios for the slaughtering of the cat. One image in particular comes to mind: The dead cat is lying on its back on a tree stump, its stiff limbs sticking out to all sides. Standing next to it is a woman wrapped in several layers of scarves and lifting an ax high in the air.

The event took place during the Second World War. There have been numerous other wars and misfortunes since then, but our personal misfortune was the siege of Leningrad during World War II. The city was surrounded by German troops, and no one could enter or leave it. People everywhere were overtaken by death during that 900-day siege, in which it is said that 2 million people died from starvation. The exact figure is unknown. My mother survived.

She had a good friend who had a brother. They were all three in Leningrad during the siege. On February 15, 1942 the temperature outside was thirty degrees Celsius below zero. The city was freezing from cold and starved out. Nothing was working, neither the water supply, nor electricity or public transport.

People fetched water from the Neva River, but not everyone had the energy to carry it home. Some would collapse on their way back and freeze to death. You could go to bed in your own home and risk falling asleep for all eternity. People also died at their workplaces. At first, they would be buried in a coffin, but as the number of deceased increased it became more common to wrap them in a sheet or blanket and later on in whatever clothes they happened to have been wearing at the time of their death. At a cemetery, which had been selected to serve that particular purpose, dynamite had been used to blast large holes in the frozen ground. These holes were expanded until they were twenty-five meters long, three meters wide, and two and a half meters deep. Mass graves, down into which the dead were dumped. A man was walking around down in the graves, poking here and there at the lifeless corpses to make sure they were placed correctly. After a while, people became so feeble that they didn't have the energy to drag their dead to the cemetery. So the corpses would be left on the street for others to transport them to the mass graves.

On that particular day, February 15, 1942, the month in which the death toll, combined with the death toll for the month of January, had reached its highest during the entire siege, the brother of my mother's friend caught a cat. Instead of devouring it all alone, he invited my mother to share it together with him and his sister. One of them had a drop of castor oil for frying it, another some dried onion peels, and the third had the cat itself. All three of them survived and were thereby not included in the list of the 199,187 people who died during the months of January and February in 1942. They survived the entire 900 days of starvation, and for the rest of their lives they would celebrate "The Day of the Cat" every year. They were true friends.

On February 15, 1956, I was twelve years old. Back then, my name was Sofa Drissen. Sofia/Sofa/Sonya/Sonyechka were still one and the same person. Later, when I moved to Denmark, it became apparent that "sofa" was a piece of furniture (a couch). My surname, Drissen, sounded uncommonly close to the Russian word for diarrhea. So, in 1956, on the "Day of the Cat," I, "Shitty Couch," stood in the shared kitchen space of our big apartment where seven other families lived, observing my mother as she prepared for the evening's festivities.

We lived in a "communal apartment," a phenomenon that arose after the revolution when big luxury flats were divided up into small rooms so that many families could inhabit them. There were eight rooms in our apartment and twenty-eight people all in all. One side of the apartment faced a wonderful street in what, to our eyes, was the most beautiful city in the world. The other side faced a courtyard. The rooms were very different from one another. Some families had a big room, while others a smaller one. It was completely random who got what. However, each family only got one room, which all led out to a long, narrow hallway with a lavatory at the end; a teeny tiny room with a flush toilet upon which one sat majestically on a slight elevation. Newspaper that had been cut into square pieces, slightly bigger than ordinary pieces of toilet paper, hung from a nail on the wall. The paper was rather hard, so you had to crumble it tightly to make it softer. At that time, there was no such thing as toilet paper in the Soviet Union, and even later, when it became a more ordinary household item, it could still be hard to come by.

Halfway down the hallway, a telephone hung on the wall. V33745 was our common telephone number. There was also a bathroom with a tub, but it wasn't easy to use because you had to heat it with firewood, which was rather scarce. Getting the water heater to work was a slow process, and as a result we usually preferred going to the public bath. However, you could wash your clothes there—and talk with your friends if you wanted to have a private conversation.

There was one kitchen with eight kitchen counters, one for each of the housewives. Soups galore were prepared shoulder to shoulder. Eight housewives exchanged recipes with one another, borrowed salt from one another, and commented on the course of events within our many walls. The food was prepared on two and a half stoves: two stoves with four burners on each and one with two. Each family had a designated burner, which they were responsible for keeping clean. If more were needed, you would have to knock on someone's door and ask if you could borrow one. That day in 1956, my mother was given permission by our best friends in the apartment, a family consisting of a father, a mother, and three daughters, who had dibs on the use of the oven, to borrow it in order to bake a Napoleon cake.

The family of five had the biggest room, a whopping twenty-five square meters. They couldn't possibly ever hope to attain a bigger one. Back then, the only way you could line up in the system's queue for new living quarters was if you had less than four and a half square meters per person.

The equation for a five-member family looked like this:

$$5 \text{ m}^2 \times 4½ \text{ m}^2 = 22½ \text{ m}^2$$

$$25 \text{ m}^2 - 22½ \text{ m}^2 = 2½ \text{ m}^2$$

Which meant they had 2½ m² too much space.
Too bad for them!

My mother, father and I had 12 square meters and qualified for 13½ square meters.

Our equation looked like this:

$$3 \times 4½ \text{ m}^2 = 13½ \text{ m}^2$$

We had 1½ m² too little space. What luck!

We were subject to the system's pettiness. We were allotted a half square meter, a half hour, half a torment. In this way, you would wait for eons to get permission to queue up for a better place to live. When you finally got that permission, a new waiting period would begin. Twenty years could easily pass, and you would still be signed up in the waiting list, until you finally were allotted that place to which you had actually been entitled to all those years.

We would be eight people at the party—those who had survived and their families. Here sat the people who had saved each other's lives back then, the residuals of the siege, each one with their own account of how they survived, each story more frightening than the next.

There was the story of my grandfather who became crazy and screamed himself to death when he received his ration of sugar for a month and ate the whole thing in one go. As a child, I would get the story all mixed up. Had he eaten the sugar because he had already gone crazy from starvation, or did he go crazy when he realized he had eaten all the sugar?

And then there was the story about my aunt, my mother's sister. She had been pregnant and had to give birth when the worst of the cold weather had announced its arrival in 1942. She staggered through the snow to the birth clinic, where she was placed on a table. She was forced to keep her coat on in order not to freeze to death. The child was born, came out from the warmth and into the cold, and died. She sat holding it in her arms for a long time before anybody came to remove the corpse from her. Then she got on her feet and, with blood hanging as brown chunks of ice on her coat, she walked back to the military camp where she worked. There were some sailors assigned to the camp. Their ship was ice bound in the Gulf of Finland and couldn't budge out of the ice. Each sailor gave her a spoonful of soup, which added up to a whole plateful.

She never got any more children. But that was only to my benefit—I got an extra mother. I can still see her beautiful hands before me. She always made circular circling motions with them whenever she spoke about the siege. She was on the verge of dying from starvation at one point and was lying in her room, which was dark and cold. Most of the windows in the city had been shattered from the pressure of the exploding bombs. She lay dreaming about bread, about Russian rye bread, which is round. She caressed it. Stroked the non-existing bread in circling motions. At this point, my mother had managed to attain an extra ration of meat of 26.6 grams and a piece of fat weighing 8.3 grams. The meat was a tiny piece of liver, which she carried with her across the city to give to my aunt. For me, the siege is the sight of my aunt making motions with her hands as she told the story about the bread that only existed in her imagination, about her little sister who ventured out on a long journey to bring her that little piece of life-saving liver.

Back to February 1956. How do you give a party for eight people in a twelve-square-meter room, which already houses a couch, a table, four chairs, a chest of drawers, and an upright piano? It's just as simple as putting four elephants in a Volkswagen: you put two in the front seat and two in the backseat.

We called our room the "trolley car." It was two meters wide and six meters long, and had a window opposite the door. The window faced a dark courtyard, a typical courtyard in Leningrad that is often described in classical Russian literature. If I leaned out far enough and looked toward one of the six-story buildings on the other side of the courtyard, I could discern whether or not a ray of sun was reflected on its wall. In that way, I could determine what the weather was like. The window was also our refrigerator. During the winter we would hang our food out the window from a bag, and in the summer we would place the food between the two window panes since the sun never reached that far down into the courtyard anyway.

There was room for four people on the couch if you sat very close together, and there could be at least another four around the dining table in front of the sofa. There was always room for everyone. You served whatever food you had managed to procure that day. Everything would be put out all at once. A Russian celebratory meal does not consist of an appetizer, a main course, or a final desert.

Herring would always be served. In Denmark you eat it spiced or marinated, that is, cured herring, but in Russia you would eat salted herring, and you still do. Chopped herring with onions, sour cream, and an apple, if you managed to get one, was also included in the menu. Next, a salad consisting of meat, potatoes, eggs, pickles, green peas, and mayonnaise.

You would often wonder how it was possible to get a hold of all these delicious dishes placed before you on the table. The most sought-after products, mayonnaise and green peas, were always a problem. The lines for eggs, meat, and fruit were endless. You would get in behind the last person standing in line and ask, "What is it we are standing in line for here?" If, for example, it was eggs right at that time, and you could get ten per person, I would stand in line with my mother because that way we could get double the amount. Bread could easily be purchased in the big cities, but if you were out in the countryside you would have to stand in line in the middle of the night in order to get it.

It was easy to control people who had to use all of their free time to stand in line to get food. You would sometimes wonder whether those in power deliberately deprived the people of certain food products. You could almost imagine a Party secretary thinking, "They must stand in line at all costs, so we'll make them stand in line for green peas and mayonnaise." Well, that's an absurd thought. But to this very day I still can't fathom why it was those two particular items that the Soviet Union was unable to produce in large quantities.

You didn't need mayonnaise or green peas to make a Napoleon cake. However, the cake was time consuming and difficult to make because you had to bake a lot of thin layers. My mother would bake it only once a year: on "The Day of the Cat."

Under the siege, in the coldness and the darkness, she had passed the time by copying down recipes from a cookbook into a small notebook she had. It is a wonderful cookbook that was published before the revolution.

Home and Housekeeping
A Guide to Proper Housekeeping in the City
and in the Country
St. Petersburg, 1909

Nutritionally balanced food recipes
Distribution of game, fish, and vegetables throughout the year according to the seasons including descriptions of dishes for special occasions.

February:
Game: Blackcock, snipe, hazel grouse, and pheasant hen.
Fish: perch, Pike perch, salmon, bream, pike, and carp.
Vegetables: Same as in January.

List of Dishes

Sunday

Dishes for fine dining: Turtle soup. Steamed pike. Pheasants with sour pickles. Orange ice cream.

Simple dinner dishes for six people: Broth with rice croquettes. Stuffed brisket of veal with potato salad (purchase one quarter of a calf: as roast, use half of the breast with the cutlet part, the neck and legs are used for the broth). Lemon pudding with cream.

Monday

Fine dining: Broth with little pies. Ox tongue with chervil. Roasted hen with cranberry. Poundcake with raspberry jam.

Simple dining: Soup with cheese. Three-pound brisket of beef. Pork chops with white beans (2½–3 pounds of pork chops, one pound beans soaked overnight).

Tuesday

Fine dining: Bouillon à la Jardinière. pike perch in capers sauce. Fillet of beef in Madeira sauce. Custard ring.

Simple dining: Yellow peas (six jars of peas, two pounds of pork). Juicy meat (leftovers from Sunday placed directly into boiling water).

Wednesday

Fine dining: Celery soup with meatballs. Sausage with sweetened brown cabbage. Roast lamb à la Finansière with endive salad. English plum pudding with eggs whipped with sugar.

Домъ и Хозяйство

Руководство

къ раціональному веденію домашняго хозяйства

въ городѣ и въ деревнѣ.

С.-ПЕТЕРБУРГЪ.

1909.

Питательные кухонные рецепты.

Распредѣленіе дичи, рыбъ и овощей по мѣсяцамъ, сообразно времени года, и роспись блюдъ на особые случаи.

ФЕВРАЛЬ.

Дичь.

Глухари и тетерьки, бекасы и рябчики, дикія утки, самки фазановъ.

Рыбы.

Караси, окуни, судаки, лососина, лещи, навага, щуки, карпы.

Овощи.

Те же, что и въ январѣ.

Роспись кушаній.

Обѣды изъ тонкихъ блюдъ	Обѣды изъ простыхъ блюдъ на 6 человѣкъ
Супъ въ родѣ черепашьяго. Загнутая щука. Фазаны съ корнишонами. Апельсинное мороженое.	Бульонъ, къ нему форточная изъ риса. Начиненная телячья грудинка съ картофельнымъ салатомъ. (Покупаютъ 1/4 теленка; для жаркого берутъ половину грудинки вмѣстѣ съ котлетной частью; шею и ногу употребляютъ для бульона). Лимонный кисель со сливками.
Чистый бульонъ съ пирожками. Кервель съ бычачьими языками. Жаркое изъ куръ съ ночной брусникой. Песочный тортъ съ малиновымъ вареньемъ.	Супъ съ сыромъ (3 фунта говядины отъ грудины). Свиныя котлеты съ бѣлыми бобами (21/2-3 ф. котлетъ, 1 ф. бобовъ; бобы слѣдуетъ намочить съ вечера холодной водой).
Бульонъ à la jardinière. Судакъ подъ соусомъ изъ каперсовъ. Говяжье филе подъ соусомъ изъ мадеры. Сливочное желе.	Супъ-пюре изъ желтаго гороха (6 стакановъ гороху, 2 фунта свинины). Мясо въ соку. (Мясо, оставшееся отъ воскресенья, опущенное для варки прямо въ кипятокъ).
Подправленный супъ изъ сельдерея съ фрикадельками. Брауниколь съ сосисками. Жаркое изъ баранины à la financière, къ нему салатъ индивій. Англійскій плумъ-пуддингъ съ сабайономъ.	Супъ изъ сельдерея, пирогъ (3 ф. грудины). Бифштексъ съ картофельнымъ салатомъ (21/2 фунта говядины филе).
Чистый бульонъ съ пирогомъ. Сладкіе коренья съ копченой гусиной грудинкой. Бекасы, къ нимъ салатъ изъ тыквы. Малиновое желе.	Щи (3 фун. говядины отъ огузка или отъ бедра). Говядина съ картофелемъ и соусомъ изъ хрѣна. Вафли съ вареньемъ.
Подправленная уха. Фаршированная капуста. Тушеное въ уксусѣ мясо съ зеленымъ горошкомъ. Яблоки à la Pompadour.	Борщъ (5 фун. бедры, худшіе куски на супъ, лучшіе на зразы). Зразы съ морковью.
Супъ изъ вина. Макароны въ формѣ съ вареной ветчиной. Тетерка съ солеными огурцами. Вареники изъ сливъ.	Супъ изъ свинины съ перловой крупой (21/2 фун. свинины). Шнельклопсъ (21/2 фунта филе) съ картофелемъ.

Холодныя закуски.

Голландскія селедки. Сардинки. Миноги. Винегретъ. Вареная ветчина. Майонезъ изъ лососины. Рулетъ изъ щуки. Рябчики. Ростбифъ. Маринованные огурцы. Брусничное варенье. Кремъ изъ апельсиновъ. Желе изъ вина (улей).

Вина: шерри, мадера, портвейнъ, шато-д'икемъ, шато-лафитъ.

Simple dining: Celery soup, pies (three-pound brisket of beef). Beef with potato salad (2½-pound fillet of beef).

Thursday

Fine dining: Bouillon with pies. Breast of goose with root vegetables. Snipes with pumpkin salad. Raspberry custard ring.

Simple dining: Cabbage soup (three pounds beef). Beef with potatoes and horseradish sauce. Waffles with jam.

Friday

Fine dining: Fish soup. Stuffed cabbage. Meat simmering in vinegar with green peas. Apples à la Pompadour.

Simple dining: Borscht (five pounds beef, the less favorable parts to be used in the soup and the most favorable in the Danish fried meatballs). Fried meatballs with carrots.

Saturday

Fine dining: Wine soup. Baked macaroni with boiled ham. Grey hen with salted cucumbers. Ravioli with plums.

Simple dining: Pork soup with pearl barley (2½ pounds of pork). Fillet of beef (2½ pounds of fillet) with potatoes.

> *Cold appetizers: Dutch salted herring. Sardines. Little eels. Beetroot salad. Boiled ham. Salmon mayonnaise. Steamed pike. Snipes. Roast beef. Pickled cucumbers. Cranberry jam. Orange cream. Wine jelly.*
>
> *Wine: Sherry, Madeira, Port wine, Château d'Yquem, Château Lafite.*

My mother was born just before the revolution and had neither seen a blackcock nor a female pheasant. That whole lifestyle, with the landed gentry, servants, and pheasant hens disappeared after the revolution.

For Tuesday, February 15, 1942, it was recommended, if it was fine dining you were after, that you consume broth à la Jardinière, pike perch with capers sauce, a filet of beef in Madeira sauce, plus custard ring as a dessert. If you were the fortunate member of the servant classes, you would on that day enjoy yellow pea soup (six glasses of peas to a pound of pork), and afterward juicy beef (leftovers of the roast stew from Sunday placed directly into boiling water). That same evening in a Leningrad that was thoroughly frozen solid, without light or heat, my mother and her two friends consumed a meal fit for a king consisting of a cat fried in castor oil garnished with three dried onion peels. On that day, 30,000 people died from starvation in the city.

One day, twenty years later, I made Danish meatballs for my mother and me, a whole frying pan of them, fourteen in all. Then I went out and came back a few hours later. When I looked into the refrigerator, they were all gone. I asked my mother what had happened to them. Shaking her head, she looked at me like a guilty dog. She knew she had done something wrong, but her feelings had overpowered her, and she confessed, "I ate them." "Did you eat all fourteen meatballs?"

It grew quiet. Then she answered, "I suddenly got worried that they might spoil." The mania of starvation struck at the oddest moments even twenty years later.

In our communal apartment, the dining table abounded with dishes. There was mayonnaise, there were green peas, and a Napoleon cake. The guests sat squeezed together in front of the food, some at the edge of the sofa, so that there was room for me behind them. I was lying with my nose in a book and was perfectly content.

Throughout my entire childhood, my parents tried to stuff me with food but I didn't want it. It wasn't until I was a grown-up that I understood why they had tried to force me to eat. It was their eternal fear: that there wouldn't be enough food. That evening they laughed and sang with their guests. Most likely, I was the only one who thought a lot about the cat. The others were just happy to be alive.

Eating was an eternal torture for me. It wasn't because I was in any way anorexic, I just didn't feel like eating all that food my mother was determined to serve the family every day. And you were expected to eat it with bread, too. Nowadays it is common around the world to tell children to finish up everything on their plate. When I myself had a daughter, I didn't forget the solemn promise I had made to myself: never, ever to force my own child to eat more than she wanted to. When I started bottle-feeding her and she every so often took a break from sucking on the bottle, I thought it was because she didn't want anymore and so I'd put it away. That, of course, resulted in her sucking on the bottle like crazy until it was completely empty from then on. Whereupon she would look at me with big, expectant eyes, as if asking, "Will more be coming? Which made me think of the long trail reaching from the starvation in Leningrad in the 1940s to Copenhagen in the mid-1970s.

The daily food ration in Leningrad in 1942 was 125 g of bread. Period.

Dog Doing Well

It was the end of the summer 1952, shortly before I was to start the first grade. We had been visiting my aunt in Lithuania, where I had been bitten by a dog. A cute little dog who had unwittingly snapped at me as we were playing and broke my skin. I felt bad for the dog, of course, but I was the one who ended up suffering for it by having to receive forty injections in my stomach for quite some time. Against rabies. When we returned to Leningrad after the visit, I continued to receive the injections.

At that point, Stalin had eight months left to live. In the course of twenty years he had managed to kill millions of people with the help of the KGB monster. Workers and farmers, soccer players and archaeologists, high or low status. When he and Hitler divided Europe between them in 1939, Lithuania became Stalin's part of the loot. Six years later, the war was over, though it wasn't entirely over. Lithuanian partisans hid in their native forests in an attempt to defeat the almighty Soviet Union. They would strike whenever they could. And so did Stalin. The massacres continued.

My mother and I were busy getting me ready to start school. She sewed small pockets made of green felt, which were joined together to make a long piece of fabric. In each pocket there was a square piece of cardboard, upon which I had drawn in bright colors one of the letters of the Russian alphabet. But I had learned the whole thing by heart long ago. There were thirty-three of them in the Russian alphabet. I was living in a whirling stream of letters.

Every day we would walk past the school, a pink building on Leo Tolstoy's Square. My sense of anticipation grew greater and greater the closer we got to the first day of school. However, whatever joy and excitement I felt at starting first grade was overshadowed by the fact that my mother often cried and had tremendous concerns. Here, in the late summer of Stalin's despotism, persecutions of the Jewish minority were becoming a daily event. People started disappearing once again. Because my mother was Jewish, she was fired from her job at a chemical research institute and couldn't get another one. Instead, she had to make her living as a manicurist. Despite the murders committed against their uncles, aunts, husbands, sweethearts, brothers, and sisters, women still needed to get their hair and nails done.

One day she received a phone call and—without any explanation—was summoned to report to the post office. Why the post office?! The most peaceful of places! And no one we knew had ever been summoned to the post office. When people got arrested, it was either at their homes at night, at their workplace, or on the street. I remember her dread and I had no idea what she was so afraid of.

She packed a bag of winter clothes, locked the door of our room, and took me along, past the pink-colored school building, the Culture House, past the women who stood selling flowers on the sidewalk. We arrived at the post office. There was a strong smell of sealing wax there. People were standing in line waiting to deliver packages at one window, deliver and receive letters at another, and at a third window they were paid their pensions. We were led past them and into the back premises, where two men sat waiting for us. One of them placed a telegram, which had arrived from Lithuania, on the table in front of my mother. "What does this mean?" he demanded.

Tears started running down my mother's cheeks. My mother read aloud: "Dog doing well." Just those three words, nothing else, because every word cost money. She stared uncomprehendingly at the telegram and started to sob. Though what could be so incomprehensible? "Dog doing well," she repeated. Obviously! My aunt had gotten the dog examined and it turned out to be fully and completely healthy. I didn't need any more injections. And it wasn't an encrypted message in any way either. My mother was neither a spy nor an enemy of the people and didn't have any connections to the rebel group in the Lithuanian forest. The Soviet Union had nothing to fear.

She looked at the two as she continued to weep, but now the meaning had finally dawned on her and she started explaining it to them. She said to me, "Sonyechka, sweety, show them your tummy." I readily pulled up my shirt so that they could properly see the many bruises I had from the injections. How lucky for us that I had come along!

Miraculously, we were allowed to leave. The warm clothes that my mother had brought wouldn't be needed after all. When we got out onto the street she stopped in her tracks and started laughing as the tears ran down her cheeks. "Fools!" she cried out. I remember her laugh. She laughed all the way home.

This was my first encounter with the monster when it thrashes its tail. It was also the time when my family got a new motto: "Dog doing well," we would always say when there wasn't anything to fear.

Lolita Torres

The Venice of the North. The city that Peter the Great founded at the mouth of the Neva River in the Gulf of Finland. The most beautiful city in the world with the gray laced waves demarcated by pastel-colored palaces and built by the finest Italian architects. St. Petersburg—Petrograd—Leningrad—St. Petersburg. Call it what you want. Same city. My city.

From the bridge across the Neva, the street meandered toward the house, number 27, that was situated right by Leo Tolstoy's Square. A beautiful glass-framed section adorned the entire front door. Inside one encountered a princely entrance lobby with a fireplace and wall paintings. The fire in the fireplace had gone out during the revolution together with the concierge—and none of them had ever returned.

A broad, worn marble staircase led to the apartments of the five-story building. Our apartment was on the second floor. There were eight doorbells lined up in a row outside the door, one for each family who were all in the same boat sailing toward the same joyous future of communism.

So many people living together under the same roof could easily have turned into a living hell, but we all lived in peace and tolerance, despite the fact that we kept an eye on one another's doings and an ear on one another's telephone conversations. Each of us knew what the others ate, how often they bathed, who slept with whom, how often they went to the bathroom, which was situated at the bottom of a long dark hallway next to the kitchen, and who spoke on the phone with whom. And so everyday life continued its habitual course among the passengers on the cruise towards communism.

You took turns cleaning the common areas without any particular drama. When it was our turn, my job was to cut out newspapers into small squares, which were to be hung on nails attached to the bathroom wall. It was impressed upon me several times that there were to be no pictures of faces on any of them. Imagine if you accidentally put a picture of Stalin on the nail and ended up drying your behind with it!

In a gigantic sixteen-square-meter room, right across from ours, lived an elderly couple and their grown-up son. The man was erect, gray-haired, and up in years. He was extremely polite, always greeting you kindly and always gallantly holding the door open for women. He had been "something" before the revolution, but it was never mentioned what that "something" had been. Even though we lived so closely together, we didn't know everything about one another, one always feared unpleasant revelations. In every communal apartment there was a representative among the residents through whom the authorities communicated. The polite gentleman was our representative.

He was married to a woman who didn't dare venture out during the day. Sometimes, after the rest of us had gone to bed, my mother would say, "I'm just going down with Nina Sergeevna," whereupon she would escort the woman down the stairs and out into the courtyard. Such a courtyard was known as a "well" in Russian because there were buildings on all sides that crowded a small space, giving you the feeling of being at the bottom of a well. My mother took the woman by the arm and walked around with her in the dark for a little while. It was before the knowledge of phobias.

In the biggest room in the entire apartment, which was twenty-five square meters, lived a father, a mother, and their three daughters. They were the ones who had two and a half square meters too much space and so they weren't able to apply for new living quarters. In Leningrad at that time you were only permitted to enter the queue for new living quarters if you had less than four and a half square meters per person. One of the daughters was my age, and we were the youngest of the crew members.

The oldest daughter got married, so the closet in the family's room was pushed out from the wall and into the room. The newlyweds moved in behind the closet. This is what the equation looked like after the oldest daughter got married:

> Mother, father, two unmarried daughters, 1 married daughter + husband.
>
> $6 \times 4\frac{1}{2} \text{ m}^2 = 27 \text{ m}^2$
>
> $25 \text{ m}^2 - 27 \text{m}^2 = 2 \text{ m}^2$ too small!

Hence, the family was now permitted to enter the queue for new living quarters.

Then the other daughter got married, and the inhabitants of the whole apartment held their breath. Was her husband also moving in? But alas, they moved to the husband's family and so the equation came out as before, just with a few minor adjustments:

> Mother, father, 1 unmarried daughter, 1 married daughter + husband
>
> $5 \times 4\frac{1}{2} \text{ m}^2 = 22\frac{1}{2} \text{ m}^2$
>
> $25 \text{ m}^2 - 22\frac{1}{2} \text{ m}^2 = 2\frac{1}{2}$ damn square meters too much!

So the family wasn't permitted to apply for new living quarters after all.

The Soviet society was vertical when it came to status. If you had a job as a nuclear physicist, you were light years from the level of a kindergarten teacher. Even though there was a materialistic difference between the two positions, it wasn't as much as you might have assumed. In the Soviet Union everyone constantly knew who was on top, who was at the bottom, and who was in the middle. No revolution could ever alter that fact. The dream of total equality for all proved to be a farce. All you ended up doing was changing the vertical line so that others now replaced those who had previously sat at the top, at the bottom and in the middle. There were various ways of being unequal: you could be poorer or richer, dumber or smarter, more or less dangerous. And it was all just a bunch of symbolic idiocy!

The family with the three daughters struggled hard to make ends meet. The father's occupation was a mystery to me. Not until many years later did I accidentally discover that he was a waiter—a job like any other, and yet not. It was one of the more shameful professions, and we pretended that we didn't know each other on the day that I happened to walk into the cafe in which he worked. The revolution hadn't changed a damn thing.

May was drawing to a close, and Leningrad exploded with a scent of lilacs. The school year was almost over. The summer vacation was just about to begin and would last for three months, three joyful months: June, July, and August. We started getting ready to leave for the summer.

That summer our vacation started off rather dramatically. The mother of the family with the 2½ square meters too much space at one point somehow got a hold of a roll of black woolen material. It could potentially be the start of a new life, and the possibilities were endless. Dreams of prosperity began to take shape as the material was cut into squares and blue flowers with green leaves were painted on each of them. The squares were transformed into scarves... many scarves that could be sold. You could get rich. You could find yourself at the edge of the law. You could go to jail. You could go to jail for painting blue flowers with green leaves on scarves and selling them.

Under communism, everyone had to be gloriously happy: "From each according to his ability, to each according to his needs." But at that point we were still in the socialist phase where everyone was to contribute according to their ability and receive according to the work they performed. The path to communism was paved by way of socialism, and according to that reality there was no room for private initiatives. The authorities distributed everything. The people couldn't do anything to improve their lot. Only the authorities were allowed to sell a pair of pants or a scarf. We lived in the implementation phase, on our way toward happiness, already halfway on the road to communism.

> Soviet citizens were promised that under communism they would be given everything, even their own airplanes. But what in the world would you do with one? Well, let's say you lived in Leningrad and you were told that on the main street in Moscow there happened to be some sausages for sale in a shop. You could just grab your plane, fly to Moscow, and get in line.

There was a constant sense of terror quietly lurking under the surface of reality. There were so many things that were forbidden, and everyone had something to hide. Who would report whom? In our apartment, twenty-eight people lived in a mine field in which you jumped in and out of secrets and prohibitions. In the room that was situated between us and the family of five, there lived a woman whom I thought was very nice, but somehow I also knew that I had to be a little bit careful with her. Whether I had been told that she was an informer, or whether I just had a hunch that she was, I don't know, but... might she get wind of the scarves?

This is where our summer vacation entered the picture. Obtaining food products was hard enough in the city, but once you got out into the countryside it was practically impossible. For that reason, the trip was a serious endeavor because you had to collect enough supplies to take with you. My mother started stocking up on food supplies and had a box in which she stashed them. It already contained flour, pasta, sugar, and cookies. And some candy. Not for me, but for some gypsy children. If anyone was at the bottom of society, it was the gypsies. Not far from where we were going, a whole bunch of them were packed together in a barrack.

My mother was a friend in need in the mine field. So the forbidden scarves were put in the box and concealed under all the food supplies. My mother's crime within the crime was revealed not by the informer but by my father. He had been a member of the Communist Party since 1931. He became furious, and it immediately developed into a huge scandal in our family. He screamed and shouted. My mother behaved like a partisan caught by the Gestapo during the War and wouldn't reveal where the scarves came from. I knew, but kept my mouth shut, and my father never found out. But he demanded that the scarves immediately be removed. Off we went to the countryside.

Many city dwellers would go to the countryside during the summer. To a *dacha*, the phenomenon which is also well-known in classical Russian literature. *Dacha* means "summer house." It was a place as well as a state of mind. Before the revolution, Russian society consisted of the wealthy class who resided on their estates in the countryside during the summer and moved into the city during the winter—the tsar to his Winter Palace—and a multitude of serfs without rights, in reality slaves, who lived in the countryside. There were also city dwellers who didn't have their own estates but wanted to move the family out into the country during the summer. They were known as *dachniki*. They would rent a *dacha* out in the countryside not far from the city so that the father of the family could come visit after working hours. *Dachniki* could be more or less wealthy, but they certainly weren't poverty-stricken. There emerged around them an entire infrastructure consisting of milkmaids, watchmen, stablemen, boatswain, nannies, and all sorts of other service functions, which the local peasant population provided. Their relationship to the *dachniki* was one of both fear and deference.

After the revolution, there were no more estates and no stablemen. The Russian *dacha* with which I was familiar was an entirely different phenomenon. The peasants out in the countryside still didn't have any rights and were now living in *kolkhozes* (collective farms) with the authorities as their commander-in-chief. Each district had a Party Committee, which ordered, among other things, when the planting and harvesting was to take place. Those of us who came from the city and out into the freedom of the countryside to spend our summer vacation would rent rooms with these families who, when it came right down to it, were still slaves.

Still, they were surrounded by a vast amount of nature which we could only dream of in the city. Suddenly I could wake up in the morning and immediately know whether the sun was shining. It was no longer necessary for me to lean far out of the window in order to catch sight of a ray of sunshine. You discovered that you were an entirely different animal when you were out in the country. You could live off of mushrooms and berries from the forest and drink milk from a cow whose name you would know. You could touch a flower and lie in the grass. In the city it was strictly forbidden to walk on the grass in the parks. There were signs everywhere with admonitions such as "Do not crush the grass." In a *dacha*, on the other hand, everything was permitted.

Every year we would travel to a place which was approximately a five-hour train ride from Leningrad, close to one of the oldest towns in Russia: Pskov. The journey that we took wasn't merely geographical. It was also a voyage back in time. We took a time machine from Varshavsky Train Station in Leningrad, and five hours later we found ourselves one thousand years in the past. There was no electricity. No gas. No running water in the houses. Nothing in the shops.

My mother had a sister who had a husband who had a brother who had a son whose wife had an aunt who had a son. In other words, that son was a very distant relative of ours. He finished his studies as a surgeon when he was twenty-four, whereupon he was to be stationed somewhere else for the next three years, the way things always turn out when no strong argument can be invented for one's remaining in Leningrad. The government administrated everything according to its needs, and so he was sent back in time to this village. He lived with a local family together with his young wife, who was a pediatrician. The young couple were good friends of ours, and that's why we traveled back to that village to spend our vacation several years in a row.

We rented a room with a family in a small wooden house. My father remained in the city. The young doctors were the local intelligentsia, and their home was filled from top to bottom with the complete works of various authors in green and brown jacket covers. Summer after summer, I would lie on my back with a book in my hands, reading my way through all of world literature translated into Russian: Balzac, Zola, Anatole France, Jack London, Mark Twain, Oscar Wilde, George Bernard Shaw.

When the ice age of Stalinism started to melt, there was a brief moment in the history of the country when the rulers entered a temporary ceasefire with the people. Life seemed to brighten somewhat. Out in the country it was now permitted to own a cow, which was liberating for the struggling rural population who, aside from having to provide for the rest of country, also had to keep themselves alive. All the land was still owned by the government that allotted specific places where one could mow grass for the cows' winter feed. But the hay stacks were standardized, and there was never enough. Concealed by the darkness of the night, the women would sneak out at late hours in order to supplement what was needed. With sickles in their purses, they would wander for several kilometers in order to cut grass from the edges of ditches, woods, and glades. That was the reality of communism. You forbade the people to own a cow, you allowed them to own a cow, you forbade them grass, you allowed them grass. Everyone was constantly busy trying to determine what was forbidden and what wasn't. When the authorities above had opinions about what was best for the country's people and how they could make all of mankind happy, a tiny man would be sitting in a corner just wanting to own a cow.

Times had changed when we started spending our vacations in the village. Not much, but the family had now been permitted to collect more grass, which was stored in hay lofts. However, there was still hardly anything in the shops. You lived off of the crops of the locals' vegetable gardens, and of the milk and curdled milk products produced in their homes. The cow and the vegetable gardens were your means of survival. Everywhere you grew the same things and ate the same things: potatoes, cucumbers, cabbage, onions, scallions, radishes, and dill. You would go into the woods and pick mushrooms, cranberries, raspberries, and blueberries. A festive meal in a Soviet family would consist of fried potatoes with mushrooms and freshly salted cucumbers.

A Recipe for Russian Happiness

In just twenty-four hours you can experience a taste of Russian life with a batch of freshly salted cucumbers!

1 kg cucumbers
1 bunch of dill
Leaves from a black currant bush
3–5 cloves of garlic
1 liter boiling water
1 tablespoon of salt

Thoroughly rinse the small cucumbers, cut off the ends, and put them together with the other ingredients in a glass jar. Dissolve the salt in the boiling water and pour on top. Tighten the jar shut. Eat them the following day along with new potatoes.

Our landlord had fought in the Second World War and had returned home, disabled, missing his legs. Half a man. His life was spent on a wooden board with wheels, on which he was always sitting. Every so often, the neighbors would come to help him up to the road, where he would eagerly speak with the passers-by. Much of what others only dared to think, he would say out loud. He was fearless, he had nothing to lose.

The War was the worst tragedy in the history of the nation. Twenty-seven million[1] people lost their lives. The number of widows and orphans that resulted from it is unknown. Two million five hundred and six thousand soldiers returned home disabled and unfit for work. They put on their decorations and medals and begged on the streets and in the market squares. The still living remains of men with severed limbs rode around in the trains, where they sang and were given hand-outs. Men without legs, without arms. The blind ones. The burnt ones. At some point they disappeared. Didn't fit into the picture postcard. A smear on the military triumph. Nothing was to ruin the beautiful picture of a content, socialist society. Away with them! One and all, stock and barrel, they were rounded up and escorted out of the cities to specially established centers. Out of sight—out of mind. But not our landlord. His wife hadn't turned her half-husband away. She had welcomed him with open arms when he returned home. He was a happy man.

We left the city for the country to get some fresh air and some exposure to nature. We were *dachniki* and lived in a kind of symbiosis with the family, because people out in the country didn't receive any income. We paid for the room. We bought their vegetables. We bought milk. I was allowed to pet the cow, while this half-man of the house milked it with his strong hands. And then we would queue up together for bread.

No one baked their own bread. There was no tradition for it and there wasn't enough grain to provide for the whole country either. It was now being imported from the

---

[1] This number was revised since the original publication of the book. The current estimation of the Soviet Union's battlefield losses in the Second World War is now forty-two million.

United States and Canada. And from that grain would be produced factory bread, which was delivered once a week to the only shop in the village, where you had to stand in line all night. My mother and I took turns. One would take one half of the night, the other would take the other half. You had to be two because there were rules as to how much a single person could buy. The bread was also used as animal fodder by the local families. And so the vicious circle was complete.

The people in the countryside were to feed the rest of the nation, and therefore they were kept on a tight leash. If, as a serf of the state, one had any dreams of moving to the city, one might as well forget all about it. In order to be allowed to live in the city you had to get a passport, which had a stamp in it saying that you had a specific address in the city. The authorities refused to issue passports to the rural population, and control procedures were carried out ruthlessly.

That summer out in the country, I was almost thirteen years old. My body was changing, and I was starting to have big thoughts. Who was I? What was I going to be when I grew up? One night I had a dream.

I'm on a bus full of people and suddenly the bus stops. A German soldier steps in, armed. In my dream I know that he is looking for Jews, and on the bus I'm thinking: How can you recognize a Jew? Can you see it in a person's appearance? The soldier walks through the bus and passes me. In passing he pushes me with his rifle without looking at me. I understand that I will be thrown off the bus and killed. And I think once more: how could he tell that I am Jewish?

At school our names, nationality, chronic diseases, and absences were listed in our classroom teacher's journal. Even though the students didn't have access to the journal, we would sometimes sneak in to look at it if it was lying out on the teacher's table while he or she had stepped out for a moment. "Jew" it said under my nationality. "It HAS to say that," they said. "You are Jewish, and it HAS to say that in your class journal. It also has to say so in your passport."

Why? I didn't feel the least bit Jewish. No one spoke "Jewish" at home, neither Yiddish nor Hebrew. We didn't celebrate any Jewish holidays. No, that's incorrect! I didn't even know they existed. I didn't discover it until I was a grown-up when I was reading a book that had been translated from Yiddish. In the book there were notes explaining what, for example, "Hanukkah" was.

There were many people like me in the Soviet Union, people with a wrong label. The package was stamped with the word "Jew" in big letters. But if you opened it, a Russian would fall out—most probably, someone similar to me, someone who spoke Russian, thought Russian, read world literature in Russian, listened to German music, ate Russian food, read French novels, and as an adult loved internationally.

The subject of nationality became particularly interesting at the end of my school days. You knew that it was no use applying to a number of higher educational institutions. Jews simply weren't admitted into them. You wouldn't ask why. That was just how it was and you accepted it. But all of that was far into the future. Right now, while it was summer, I became a dove of peace.

The house in which we were renting the room was on Victory Street. The street had this same name even before the War. I often thought about which victory it referred to. The most common names for streets were Lenin's Street, Victory Street, Proletarian Street, and Revolution Boulevard. There was a Victory Street in every town, but who had been victorious over whom and when? Was it the victory over the Swedes in the eighteenth century? Napoleon in 1812? Or the time when the Reds overcame the Whites in 1922?

Our Victory Street was a gravel road. If you walked through the vegetable garden and then through a slightly marshy area, a kind of no-man's land, there was an elevation at the bottom, upon which there stood a two-story house made of stone, one of the few among all the wooden houses. That was a Culture House. Inside, there was a stage, and above the stage there hung a big red banner with a quote from Lenin: "Of all the arts, the most important for us is cinema."

There was dancing in the Culture House every Saturday. The youth of the village, the local *dachniki*, and soldiers from a nearby military unit showed up for some entertainment. That summer the Culture House was given a piano, whereupon it was decided that a concert was to be arranged before the dancing began in the evening.

At that time the country was drowning in a Lolita-mania. The first film to be purchased from the West and shown in the Soviet union after Stalin's death had been an Argentinian musical titled *The Age of Love*. Why specifically an Argentinian film? We had nothing in common in terms of culture, language nor geography. After enduring numerous years of suffering and the most unimaginable tragedies, we Russians needed to wrap ourselves in a little warmth and love.

The star of the movie was Lolita Torres. From Moscow to Vladivostok, the country was completely washed over by the mania. Daughters were named after Lolita. Women had their hair done up in the same hairdo as Lolita's. They dressed like Lolita. And the country drank Lolita songs, as dry soil drinks in the spring rain.

My mother, the youngest daughter of a rabbi, had a fantastic singing voice. She never managed to use it professionally, life had been too hard for that, but she would gladly sing for family and friends. For the concert that summer night, my mother had agreed to treat the locals by singing Lolita Torres's songs.

But you didn't dare arrange a concert consisting only of love songs. This was where I came flying into the picture as a dove of peace, one of many children dressed in costumes for the occasion. The Culture House had to be decorated, and the local choir was to sing one of the mandatory Party songs first. Love would have to nicely get in line and wait.

I was to be part of the choir. My mother drew a dove of peace from two pieces of paper, which she pasted together to make a hat. I put it on for the choir rehearsal, and we practiced singing all nine verses of *The Party is Our Helmsman*, a song which everyone was able to sing along to.

> *Glory to the fighters who stood up for truth,*
> *Those who lifted the flag of liberty that soars high above.*
> *Those who created our Party,*
> *And led us towards a common goal*
>
> *Sung twice*
>
> *Long hard years under the tsars*
> *Our people lived in bondage.*
> *Lenin showed us the dawn of Communism*
> *And, in the darkness, there came light.*

A few days before the concert, a man showed up at the host family. I thought he had the most beautiful name: Maximillian. I, the little dove, the symbol of peace, was completely spellbound. Maximillian was an ethnic German, married to the host's sister. It was the first time I had seen a German.

> Maximillian's story began 250 years earlier when Catherine the Great, a powerful female leader in Russia who was originally of German descent, inspired her German countrymen with the most dazzling prospects and invited them to Russia to boost Russian agriculture and economy. They came and lived in the cities, in the countryside, and along the Volga River for many generations.

After the revolution, an entire republic of Volga Germans was established. In the newspapers of the past, it was called *Stalin's blooming garden,* because they brought about great growth for Russian industry and agriculture. At the outbreak of the Second World War, they were all, men, women, and children, old and young, under the pretext of having to be protected from the anger of the Russian people, deported to remote areas of the Soviet Union. Thousands of kilometers away. Seven hundred and seventy-four thousand one hundred and seventy-eight completely ordinary Soviet citizens, ethnic Germans, torn up at the root, loaded onto cattle cars, and deported to Kazakhstan, the Urals, and Siberia.

The man with the beautiful name had come from far away to tell the hostess that her sister was dead. But he hadn't been given permission to leave Kazakhstan, the territory where they had been deported. He had committed a crime! For two days he stayed with the family and seldom ventured outside. For two days no one spoke out loud in the house. They whispered.

My mother, the eternal criminal, found a kindred spirit in Max. He could play the piano and was a former music teacher. The piano of the Culture House and Max showed up in the village at practically the same time. Together with my mother's golden voice, a synthesis was formed. For two days those two people spoke through the music in the stone house with the long benches. I sat in a corner together with the other children and listened to them.

The day of the concert came. It also happened to be the one day of the year when our host had to show up at the nearest hospital in order to get a medical confirmation that he was actually a disabled person. You could never be too sure. "Let's see, have my legs grown out since the last time I was here? No, I still don't have them." And so off he went to the hospital on the legs he didn't have.

In the evening his neighbors carried him to the Culture House and placed him on his board on the floor at the end of one of the rows. I was to sit next to them, between him and his wife. As a present, my mother had given her one of the many forbidden scarves with the blue flowers and green leaves, which she wore on her shoulders on this special evening. The young doctors were present, the locals, the soldiers from the military unit, and all the *dachniki*. Together with the choir I sang:

> *Under the sun, our motherland becomes stronger year by year.*
> *We remain utterly faithful to the cause of Lenin.*
> *Calling together the achievements of the Soviet people*
> *—The Communist Party of the country!*
>
> *Sung twice*

What the audience was feeling as the choir lauded the Party and everyone waited expectantly to hear the Lolita Torres songs is difficult to fully express in English. In Russian, there is a beautiful word:

> **PREDVKUSHENIE:** *It means that you look forward to, anticipate, have great expectations for something— but literally* **it means to have a taste of the future in your mouth**.

And the future was standing right in the wings. My mother and Max stepped onto the stage. Max sat down at the piano, and my mother transformed herself into Lolita:

> *When I meet your gaze,*
> *I feel a pang in my heart.*
> *When you quietly sigh,*
> *I know why.*

With my right hand, I was squeezing the hand of the disabled soldier on the wooden board, and with my left, that of his wife who was wearing the prohibited scarf. The audience sniffled.

> *For the rest of my life, before I die,*
> *I must live without you.*
> *Although my heart is begging me not to,*
> *I must ask you to leave, go your way.*
>
> *Only don't be angry, my friend,*
> *just go, farewell, my friend.*
> *Our paths were destined to cross*
> *but we must now go separate ways.*

It was impossible to live in reality in the Soviet Union. It was too painful. No matter how many atrocities the people were exposed to, the propaganda about how happy their lives were continued to boom above their heads. After Stalin's death revelations about the crimes committed by the machinery of power came to light—and suddenly, after forty years of wars, hunger, and governmental terror holes began to emerge in people's consciousness because they began to understand that they had been living a lie. And it was at that very moment that the Argentinean musicals began to be introduced, which only dealt with love. They filled the holes in people's consciousness where there had previously been slogans of communism.

The deported German and my Jewish mother led the people into a new illusion. There wasn't a dry eye in the house.

> *We have no need for glances,*
> *We have no need to touch hands,*
> *We are both doomed to tears,*
> *Doomed to suffering and memories.*

Max left that same night—and that night there was no bread to stand in line for. With the Party as our helmsman, we headed toward Lolita's comforting embrace.

"Shitty Couch" on the Wings of History

It was the happiest day of my life in the Soviet Union. It was the day when I was happy along with 220,000,000 other people. One hundred fifty nationalities, 15 republics, 11 time zones cried with joy and embraced one another in the streets.

April 12, 1961 marked the day that a human being traveled to space for the first time. It was our man, Yuri Gagarin. In 1957, the Sputnik has kindled people's expectations to reach the stars, and Gagarin could now practically touch them.

I was in the ninth grade, attending a somewhat unusual kind of school in Leningrad. My mother was already seriously disabled due to a stroke, which had left her paralyzed. Because I had to care for her full time, I was unable to attend ordinary school six days a week. I belonged to the so-called "working youth" that normally attended school at night and worked by day. However, there was one class that had instruction during the day, and I was permitted to attend it three times a week.

"How lucky I am, I have no parents." Those are the first lines of a famous novel. I could have started mine with, "How lucky I am that my mother became ill." Her paralysis made her a prisoner in her own body, a condition from which she was never to recover. On the other hand, it liberated me, however awful that may sound. It protected me from the duty of having to be an active member of the Soviet collective. School children and working people were members—and had to deal with everything this membership entailed, including control and ideological indoctrination. I managed to evade it because

I had to take care of my sick mother and therefore had an excuse not to attend ordinary school. It was at that point that I took my first steps toward a life "outside," a life, mind you, that was not considered punishable by law. On the contrary, the government had, in fact, given me permission to live that way. I was in a free space of sorts.

In the Soviet Union there was a wonderful tradition for large companies to support children's institutions. They would donate various things to schools, make sure there were sports facilities, and organize summer camps for the children. A coin factory had spread its protective wings across "The School for the Working Youth," and it was on the premises of this factory that I attended school during the day.

The coin factory was situated inside the Peter and Paul Fortress on an island in the middle of the Neva River. During the time of the tsars, the wings of the fortress were used as a jail for political prisoners. This was also the location of the cathedral in which the Russian tsars were buried. The school consisted of three rooms in the factory's administrative building, and every time I arrived I had to go through a very strict security control in order to be able to enter the area of the factory. On the opposite side of the fortress, down to the river and right in the heart of the megapolis was a beach to which the inhabitants of Leningrad would flock at the first sight of the sun in the spring.

I left the ordinary school system after a number of events that commenced when all eighth graders were sent out to the countryside. In the spring and autumn months it was customary for school classes, entire companies, university students, scientific researchers, ballet dancers, and violin players to be sent from the city to collective farms in the countryside to lend a hand. It was the most ridiculous form of farming in the history of mankind. Thousands of children picked cotton in Central Asia, thousands of others picked grapes in the Caucasian republics. We lived in the countryside for a month and weeded the fields where carrots grew. We city kids knew nothing about carrots, and I truly doubt that any carrots were able to grow on those fields after we made our contribution. I for one couldn't tell the difference between a carrot top and a weed. They should probably never have sent me out to help because Soviet agriculture never managed to feed the people.

Carrots, by the way, have continued to haunt me ever since. Years later, when I came to Denmark and had learned a little bit of Danish, my first job as a translator from Danish to Russian was for a company that exported plant seeds to Russia. The material consisted of a manual on how to plant carrots so, keep in mind, if as a consequence of that translation carrots still don't grow in Russia it is, once again, my fault.

The inefficiency of the agriculture industry was looked upon like the weather: there was nothing you could do to change it. The collectivization was implemented so brutally that no one dared question it. The farmers who weren't willing to become members of the collective farms were either executed or sent to work camps. A law had been implemented in the 1930s punished you for stealing one ear of grain from a collective farm with exile to a work camp or something even worse. The frightened farmers couldn't feed the country, and, with or without my help, the agricultural industry didn't function in the Soviet Union.

You could either laugh and cry over the absurdity of the system. And people certainly laughed. Perhaps that was the solution to the problem.

When Soviet Jews started applying for exit visas to Israel, the government came up with the most outrageous excuses. The sole purpose was to rob them of anything they possessed of value before they left the country.

> A meeting is held at a collective farm. The foreman gets up and says, "My fellow members, last year our farming industry lost a lot of money on red beets. Do you have any questions regarding this?" A man in the crowd raises his hand, "Honorable Comrade foreman, is it true that Jews that are leaving the Soviet Union have to pay a lot of money to get their exit visa?" "Yes, that is correct," the foreman confirms, "but what has that got to do with the farming industry? Let's continue. Last year our farming industry lost considerable profits on potatoes. Do you have any questions regarding this?" The same man raises his hand again, "Yes, is it true that before they leave, Jews have to pay large sums of money to the government for the education they received while living here?" The foreman answers, "Yes, that is true, but it still doesn't have anything to do with the farming industry. Let's continue. Last year we lost an exorbitant amount on carrots." Once again the same person raises his hand. The foreman says in an irritated tone, "Comrade, why do you continue pursuing this?" Whereupon the person in question answers, "Well, might I make a suggestion? Perhaps we could make a lot of money by cultivating Jews instead of carrots!"

We were two eighth grade classes, approximately eighty young people aged fourteen or fifteen, sent to a collective farm outside of Leningrad. We lived in a big barrack, ready to contribute our share but also eager to make things pleasant and cozy. Five of us were elected to be a kind of steering committee. I was one of them. It rained a lot, and we didn't spend all that much time on the carrots. Mostly we would sit in the barn and read and discuss things. This trip, as I found out many years later, proved to be ill-fated. It was precisely during that spring at the collective farm, when I was elected as a member of the committee, that the monster had picked up my scent for the first time.

There was a very clear procedure in which Soviet children were eased into the Party-faithful society in which they lived. There were three steps on this path, and if you skipped any of those steps in the course of your life you could expect problems with the state. First you were an *oktiabrionok* (child of the October Revolution), then a "Red Pioneer," and finally a "member of Komsomol" (Communist Youth League). It was the year in which we were to join the Komsomol. However, we returned to the city with a clearly formulated desire to not just automatically go through with the usual procedure when being admitted into the Youth League. Each member should be given the chance to question why they had to go through with it and the extent to which he or she even had any desire to join. It turned into a huge mutiny, which resulted in our school shutting down, with the principal dying of shock, and we were scattered to the four winds. I continued the ninth grade in the coin factory.

On April 12, 1961, I played hooky from school. The weather was simply too good to sit indoors. The ice had just broken on the Neva and people had removed their coats and stood leaning against the walls of the fortress to soak in the sun. Spring sounded like a storm bell calling to one. Instead of attending class, I strutted about the fortress grounds in my new, very stylish clothes that consisted of three pairs of repurposed pants. My father had been on a business trip to Moscow and had managed to get ahold of two pairs of thick knee-high pink underpants with a fleecy reversible side and an elastic trim produced in East Germany. The two pairs of underwear, turned inside out, were sewn into a shirt with three-quarter length sleeves and a fancy shiny button on the back. On top of that I was wearing a spencer sewn from my father's old black pants turned inside out. The pants were from Germany, in other words, of good quality. Black buttons with golden rims went all the way down. They were, however, completely new! I was extremely well-dressed and strolled around enjoying the spring weather, the river, and the beauty of the fortress.

Suddenly the loudspeakers on the surrounding masts came to life. Up until that moment, I hadn't even realized they were actually working. I thought they were a relic from the past. A familiar-sounding voice announced, "This is the All-Soviet Union Radio Station. This is the All-Soviet Radio Station." The voice roared out across the eleven time zones of the Soviet Union all at once. People stopped in their tracks. I started crying and immediately thought of the War. It was the same voice that had announced the Soviet Union's victories and defeats during the Second World War. I only recognized it from the films I had seen. It belonged to Yuri Levitan, who for almost fifty years announced the most decisive political decisions and orders on the radio. Now he was announcing that for the first time in the history of humanity a man had left our planet in a spaceship to travel into space. This was how we learned of Gagarin's space flight.

All people have experienced events which become their lodestar for the rest of their lives. Some are personal experiences, and some are shared. Kennedy's murder, the landing on the moon, September 11, the kind of experiences that create a moment in which our lives slow down. We remember the content of the moment, where we stood, what we were busy doing, how we were dressed. Time doesn't stand still in such a moment. It expands, stretches out. And I, Shitty Sofa, was on my way out into space.

I grew up with an infinite love for science fiction. I was living in a country which in itself was pure science fiction. Communism was a concept, a fiction, on which, for seventy years, tremendous effort had been spent into making it appear as a reality. We all had dreams. Sometimes the dreams turned into nightmares. The idea of communism was a concept of a better life for all of mankind. That was how it was presented. A man sent to outer space didn't just mark a patriotic victory for us, it was the dream of the entire world fulfilled before our eyes. It could happen. The dream could come true.

I had my own special and personal relationship to outer space. My favorite book was called *Aelita*, a Russian novel written right after the revolution by Aleksey Tolstoy about a space journey to the planet Mars. In brief, a Soviet engineer arrives on Mars and falls in love with a Martian girl, Aelita. He takes part in a proletarian revolution on Mars, is exiled back to Earth, and mourns his lost Martian love for the rest of his life. The novel has everything: love, space travel, Mars—and Aelita, who had her very own bedroom, which I could visualize as I lay on my foldaway bed in our twelve-square-meter room in Leningrad:

> *Aelita woke up early and lay in bed leaning on her elbow. Her broad couch, open on all sides, stood, as was the custom, on a dais in the middle of the bedroom. The dome-like ceiling terminated high up in a marble-framed skylight through which the morning light filtered into the room. The pale mosaic pattern on the wall was hidden in shadows. The shaft of light picked out only the snow-white sheets, the pillows, and Aelita's ashen head resting on her hand.*

Her own bedroom. Now *that* was science fiction!

We lived in our socialist camp and couldn't so much as even dare to hope to travel to Paris, London, New York, Tokyo, Milan. But we could dream about traveling to Mars. And Gagarin had taken the first step.

As the voice continued, I rushed back to the coin factory and through the door to the class, which was in the middle of a math lesson. I was practically choking with enthusiasm as I laughed and shouted, "A man is in outer space! A man is in outer space!" Everything stopped. Normally everything was so regimented in our lives. Now we poured out onto the streets and didn't know what to do with ourselves. People moved instinctively toward the center of the city. We walked toward the university, past the Academy of Sciences. Throngs of people came from all directions. It started looking more and more like a spontaneous demonstration.

We had never experienced anything like it on our lives. All demonstrations in the Soviet Union were always carefully planned. People would walk in organized rows on International Workers Day on May 1 and on the day of the revolution, November 7. Every hurrah was arranged by the authorities: through the loudspeakers they would shout: "Long live the Central Committee of the great Communist Party," to which the masses would respond, "Hurrah!" Whereupon the voice would again be heard through the loudspeakers, "We greet the workers at the tractor factory," to which the masses would again respond, "Hurrah!" Now, for the first time in my life I was walking through the streets together with a crowd of joyous people who hadn't been organized by an authority of any kind. Suddenly someone shouted, "Long live Gagarin!" to which we shouted "Hurrah!"

More and more people joined the crowd. We didn't know where we were going, but nevertheless ended up at the Palace Square where demonstrations were always held. For the first time people were doing something on their own initiative. For the first time it wasn't orchestrated by the authorities.

Then the militia arrived and started dispersing people. There was an attempt to divert the joy in acceptable directions. For the first time I saw what was going on: they did not want to permit unorganized mass demonstrations, not even in the name of joy.

We were the first ones in our *kommunalka* apartment[1] to get a television. It had a tiny screen with a double lens mounted on tracks, which could be pulled out to magnify the image. When I came home, I could barely open the door to the room. It was full of neighbors from the entire apartment. They were glued to the small TV in which Gagarin marched across the Red Square to submit his report to the chairman of the Communist Party of the Soviet Union.

My mother, who was paralyzed on her left side, turned her tearful face to me. They were tears of joy. She said, "Imagine that I would live to see this day. We are in outer space." She didn't say a man has traveled in space. She didn't say: "Gagarin was in outer space." She said, triumphantly, "*We* are in outer space." Our neighbors sniffled in agreement. The room radiated victory, peace, joy, and love. There we were, the Soviet people, children and grown-ups, informers and rulers, hangmen and victims. I was full of joy that night lying on my foldout bed.

Aelita, here I come!

---

1 An apartment where several families lived, each family in their room.

Sex in the Soviet Union

I got married when I was nineteen years old. With Osya, whose official name was Iosif Borisovich Nabutovsky. It is an incredibly impressive surname, Nabutovsky, and it was a great incentive for me to marry him because then I would go from being Shitty Couch to Sonya Nabutovskaya. No, of course, we also loved each other and had a child together, a son. We named him Alyosha. He died before his first birthday and we got divorced quickly afterward.

We lived in a country that had only one objective in sight: happiness for everyone. Whether rich or poor, all citizens were to be equal, free and happy, and everything was to be commonly shared across class lines. After the revolution it was not only the means of production that were to be joint property. Soviet women were in favor of their emancipation and the idea that any woman who was free and equal must also want the right to choose a husband on her own. But this was where the Soviet men were of a different mind! No, no, and, once again, no. Everything was to be common property, and we were also to be common wives. At a stormy meeting in the town of Saratov by the Volga River, with its view of the endless rolling steppes, in the midst of the Civil War, it was decreed that wives were to be considered common property. According to the declaration, from that day on, all women were to be considered the property of the state—in accordance with the very spirit of the revolution!

The revolution was a dream, a dream of paradise where no one was better than his or her neighbor and no one was richer than anyone else. A paradise on earth is quite a feat to build up, so a lot of work lay ahead. "Love is the reason why couples isolate themselves from the common collective." "Love in the form of friendship is the ideal, it is what the proletariat needs in its battle for the dictatorship of the proletariat," blared the governmental slogans. Everyone, both men and women, were, first of all, a labor force, a resource, and nothing could divert them from work. Stay focused, my friends, stay focused!

It was an impossibility. No one became emancipated and nothing became common property, not even the women. And the paradise turned into a country that justified violence and evil in the name of socialist prudence. Sex went underground together with the victims of Stalin. Sex was completely shut down under Stalin's regime of terror that lasted almost thirty years. The Caucasian dictator cultivated Victorian virtues and enjoyed the thought of innocent girls without genitals clad in straw hats with roses. Meanwhile, the soul of the country crumbled in the wind of violence. Executioners slowly crushed the genitals of their victims and thrust white hot ramrods in their anus to get them to confess that they were enemies of the people.

But rest assured, those times are thankfully over! Nevertheless, there can be no sex without genitals—and therein lies the problem. Russian is a very rich and beautiful language, but it has a kind of inbuilt embarrassment and denial. You cannot simply utter words that denote the genitals. The words themselves exist and are well known to Russian speakers. However, if you say them out loud, they turn into horribly crude, detestable curse words. As a result, the genitals are never mentioned by name. One avoids them in conversation as if they simply don't exist.

The first, last, and only time the male sex organ *khuy* had ever been translated into Danish was in a dictionary written by a Dr. Kure in 1916. It was translated as "penis" and in parentheses was added "improper." But even more improper was the female genital organ, which in Russian is *pizda*. It wasn't mentioned at all. Even Dr. Kure himself couldn't get the word past his lips. However, they did exist as unparalleled profanities.

All nations curse. You aren't supposed to say "damn" or "hell," but you do it anyway. If you try visualizing a map of the world, you will notice a vertical, slightly crooked line that runs down through Europe marking how people unite according to the profanities they use. We may disagree on a great many things, but if there is one thing that unites us it's our choice of profanities.

East of the line, the nations are united in a "sexual zone," where genitals and their functions are used as profanities. West of the line, we step into an "anal-excremental zone," in which the world is filled with assholes and everyone and everything is a bunch of "shit." Not only that, but there the Lord's name is taken in vain and people intimidate one another by referencing an afterlife in which Satan and hell reign. "Go to hell, you asshole."

Maledicere humanum est. Cursing is human. I was fortunate enough to live in a blooming world of copulating genitals in a country that was the source of all kinds of curses and oaths. It was also open to new suggestions and, therefore, not entirely averse to the concept of asses and shit. Russia is covered by a thick layer of crust concealing an ocean that seethes and bubbles with a sexual language. Every so often a hot spring erupts, finding its way out of its hiding place through a crack in the crust, as it surfaces and explodes in an emotional outburst.

Russian curse words have always lived a life of their own as a secret language, founded on sex, picturesque, coarse, offensive, but absolutely irreplaceable as a means of communication. For several generations, the language of sex has been a kind of pact that has been agreed upon in order to evade bans and censorship. It was handed down from father to son and has been incorporated into the Russian soul. A true Russian masters this language, whose speakers make up a community where they have the freedom to express themselves however they choose.

There is a host of motions that can be expressed through dicks that ceaselessly screw their mothers who are lying down passively just waiting to be violated. *Iob tvoiu mat'* was born in the sexual zone and emigrated westward, where it became "fuck your mother," broke away from the mother's skirts, and ultimately became "fuck you" and continued its victory march across the world. But the word "sex" itself was unknown to the Soviet people. After the fall of the Berlin Wall, a dictionary was published in Russian in two volumes, one consisting of 1200 possible ways to use the word "dick," the other one with 700 words for "pussy." Freedom had come to the Russian speakers.

Of course, there was a lot of sex in the Soviet Union. In the big cities, many sexual debuts often took place in stairwells. In Leningrad, within the palatial buildings where the bourgeoisie had resided prior to the revolution, the wide worn marble steps led to the top floors where there were spacious windowsills. Faded paintings and dead hearths were silent witnesses as young couples stole away to forbidden caresses.

Here, in the city situated on the same latitude as Oslo and Helsinki, the spring, autumn, and winter months were predictably cold. If one was lucky, there would be a single functioning radiator somewhere on one of the floor landings. However, its absence was no hindrance. Electrified from excitement, the male fingers would unscrew a lightbulb in the ceiling in order to feel one's way in the darkness under several layers of clothes to the inevitable fleece-lined underwear. You always ran into couples on the landings, whether it was on marble stairways, in narrow staircases with peeling walls where one encountered a whiff of the pungent stench of cat piss, or in the new residential housing in the concrete-laced suburbs. Everywhere in this Shangri-La the elevators went up and down, people walked in and out of the apartments, and children cried, while sex officially didn't exist. But where was a man to go with his poor erect dick? There was a way out!

> Excerpt from Genrikh Uzhegov's *Man's Health*, 1982
>
> Once you get used to masturbation, it is really hard to get rid of the habit. Even married men find it difficult. Masturbation is often caused by the overproduction of the sexual glands. It may also be caused by intestinal worms, hemorrhoids, or eczema.
>
> Treatments for masturbation
>
> 1. Take a cold shower in the morning and in the evening, followed by a massage.
> 2. Sleep on a hard bed and under no circumstances use a down quilt.
> 3. Eat a salad consisting of equal amounts of raw onion and parsley.
> 4. Pour one-half of a liter of boiling water over a spoonful of the catkins of a willow tree and let it infuse for an hour. Drink a glass three times a day.

The year before I married, a number of epoch-making events took place. The Soviet Union sent its first female cosmonaut into space. Before then, the female dog, Strelka, had been sent into space and had, as one of the first ones, returned to the earth alive—together with a grey rabbit, forty-two mice, two rats, and a whole bunch of flies. The whole country melted when they saw on TV that Strelka had given birth to six puppies. No one took much notice of who the father was, but here was proof that a female could be sent out into space without getting harmed by it.

It was also the year that my family took a great step into the future. We were allotted a corner apartment, a two-room apartment with a kitchen, a bath, and a small balcony situated in a concrete building, a newly constructed building complex on the outskirts of the city. We basked in the blissful light that streamed across the concrete joy and through the many windows we suddenly had been given. In the kitchen there was a stove with four burners. Our very own four burners. Imagine the food orgies we could now venture into! And on top of that, we could enjoy our meals at a table in the kitchen that was an entire five and a half square meters. It was like moving into the Winter Palace. Everywhere in the apartment the floors were covered by shiny brown linoleum upon which our new life would from now on and into the future be reflected. In the bathroom there was a toilet and hot running water. No more visits to the public bath with its crowds of naked, steaming, pink women.

The rules for obtaining a dwelling had been changed a great deal. You now had a right to nine square meters per person, double the size of what it had previously been, and the two rooms were seventeen and ten square meters. My parents got the biggest room, which also functioned as a living room. I got the smallest room. The foldout bed was thrown out, not all the way out, but just as far as the balcony. In the future it would be used for guests. I got my own sofa bed and was closer to Aelita than ever before. It was Martian joy.

Sonya woke up early and turned to the side with her hand resting beneath her head. Her new unfolded sofa bed stretched toward the morning sunlight that swept around the roofs of the cement building complex, sending sunrays through the corner window. The walls of the room—covered by pink wallpaper—remained in semi-darkness as the light fell on the snow-white bed sheets and Sonya's curly red hair.

I met Osya at work, at the research center for uniflow. The first day that I stepped into the cafeteria with my colleagues one of them said, "Look, there's Osya Nabutovsky, he's the smartest guy at this institute." "Where?" I asked, interested. And soon we were married.

I didn't want a bridal dress but got a cream colored outfit sewed for the occasion. First our marriage was registered at a civil office and afterward we went to my in-laws to drink champagne. Osya's relatives had come from far away, his was a large and devoted family many of whom I didn't know. There was too much drink and chit-chat with far too many aunts and uncles from Khabarovsk and Kharkiv. Next, we were to have a party in a rented café, but I was already very tired. When we reached the café, I asked Osya to go ahead, I would catch up later. I needed a break.

Around the corner there was a little beer kiosk the size of an overgrown telephone booth. Inside it there sat a lady dressed in a white smock surrounded by lots of large and small beer mugs, a beer tap, and a contraption in which she rinsed the mugs before using them again. Just like with everything else, you had to get in line and wait. When you had been given your beer, you would take a few steps away with your filled mug, and when it was empty you would retrace the same steps back and return it. Every now and then she would stick her head out from the small opening and shout, "Comrades, hand in your mugs, hand in your mugs."

I needed a big mug of beer in the middle all the festivities and got in line. A couple of men who had forgotten to shave in the morning were waiting to get their thirst quenched. One of them looked at me with admiration and said in a friendly tone, "What a lovely *volniashka* you are." I focused on the word "lovely" and responded that this was my wedding day. But the word *volniashka*, on the other hand, threw me a little off.

> In prison slang, *volniashka* meant a worker in a prison camp, without a military rank, for example, a teacher, driver, librarian, supplier, teamster—someone who wasn't permanently employed there but came from the outside to perform various tasks. They were often intermediaries in the legal as well as the semi-illegal exchange of goods.

In short, it was a free bird who was admitted into an otherwise inaccessible world. I couldn't have known back then that I would someday end up in Denmark and be able to fly in and out of the Soviet Union like a free bird. But this unshaven man in his mid-fifties, who had most likely been a former prisoner, appeared before me in the line to the beer kiosk that day and predicted my future.

I spent my wedding night washing my hair. Brigitte Bardot was in, which meant that the female segment of the population immediately transformed themselves, one and all, into Bardots with their hair done in teased updos. My hair was filled with loads of hair spray and tons of hair pins to keep the hairdo in place. I was totally absorbed with that and had no time for sex on my wedding night. Anyway, that had taken place at a much earlier point, even though a girl was supposed to be a virgin when she got married.

Before we got married, Osya had also lived with his parents in a single room in a big apartment with lots of neighbors. It was a long way from the stolen kisses and fumbling caresses in various random staircases of those days to now, where I was the happy owner of my very own domicile of ten square meters. Just as far as from the Earth to Mars. Osya would usually sneak into my place late at night.

One night, my mother woke up. For some reason, she went from the living room where she slept and over to my room. She opened the door but stopped abruptly when she discovered there was another person in my bed. She cried out, "Oh, you're not alone?" Osya and I held our breath, waiting for the catastrophe. But it didn't take place. My mother was a very proper person. "Forgive me," she said respectfully and closed the door.

Osya officially moved in. The morning after the wedding night we went to a jazz concert, a jam session, the first of its kind in Leningrad. It was the final years of the thaw, the mid-sixties, a time filled with music and with hope. We were told that Stalin had been a criminal and we were promised that communism would be implemented in twenty years' time. Scientific research in the Soviet Union had proven that communism was the definitive purpose of all humanity. We were living a scientifically proven fiction.

Science fiction was the most popular literary genre of our generation. In a land where all thinking floated in a communist stratum, science fiction was the only way to describe society. You simply transferred the plot to a different planet. And we were all experts at reading between the lines. We immediately recognized ourselves in a young pilot from Earth who makes an emergency landing on a different planet because something is wrong with his spaceship. The planet is ruled by a military clique that controls their society with the help of a machine located in the basement below the center of power. This machine brainwashes the entire population that ends up like robots hailing the system three times a day. However, a few members of the population remain unaffected. Instead, they get a horrible headache when the others blast out patriotic slogans. They are stamped as "monstrosities" and are either executed or sent to concentration camps to be reeducated. Our hero joins the resistance movement of the monstrosities. The machine is destroyed and all its psychic influence disappears. What happens to the population then? Half of it commits suicide, the other half lies unconscious in the deepest depression. And it turns out that those in power have mobile machines up their sleeve that take over and continue brainwashing the population. That was the plot in one of the novels by Strugatsky brothers that I greedily devoured.

Back to earth. Osya and I had a child. A son. We named him Alyosha. We were very happy. I lay for a week in Ward 31 at the maternity clinic. Osya wasn't allowed to be present during the birth and was also forbidden entry when it was over. Men were simply not permitted to enter the clinic for reasons of hygiene. They were to wait politely for their wives to be discharged a week later and escorted away from the ward by a smiling nurse who was carrying a finely decorated little "package" containing the baby in her arms.

> A man arrives at the delivery ward to pick up his wife and newborn son. A nurse says to him: "Before you get to see your son, I must tell you that he has no arms." The man cries out, "How very unfortunate. I had hoped that he would one day grow up to be a famous pianist. Oh, well, no matter, I love him anyway." The nurse continues, "But I must also tell you that he doesn't have any legs, either." The man cries out again, "How unfortunate. I had just got my hopes up that he might become a famous soccer player. Oh, well, no matter, I love him anyway." The nurse fetches a bundle that is wrapped in a blanket. The man peers down at it. There is a large pink ear lying in the blanket. He flings himself at it and says, "My son!" The nurse looks at him and says, "You'll have to speak up a little. I'm afraid he doesn't hear very well."

The gaze of my beautiful, healthy boy met mine the first time I was to feed him after the nurse had carried him into the ward. Back then, the babies were delivered to their mothers like small packages with their arms and legs wrapped closely to their bodies. From the liberty of my stomach, my son was born into a world of limitations. My little package cried until the moment he was placed in my arms and opened his eyes.

After working hours, the new fathers stood below the windows in all kinds of weather and shouted up to their wives who hung out the windows in their hospital clothes. And a lady who sat in a small glass booth received messages and packages with candy and cakes for the new mothers. The fathers would return later in hopes that there would be a response waiting for them. The possibilities to communicate with one another were limited. They could either shout or write.

Letters to and from Ward 31

> *Dear Sonya,*
> *You are wonderful! You have given birth to a son. Hurray! You know, I think I've already developed paternal feelings. I love him so much. You go ahead and start raising him without me. I'll help out later. Try counting how many fingers and toes he has. Check his intellectual capabilities and musical ear. Ask him who he likes best: Rembrandt or Cezanne. Ask him why he was so restless inside your stomach. What was it he needed? I'll provide everything. Write, little Sonya, and tell me how you feel, what his coloring is, whom he resembles, and whether you still love me.*
> *Yours,*
> *Osya*

> *Dear Osya,*
> *I only got to see the baby as I was giving birth to him so I didn't get a chance to count his fingers but I can already tell that he definitely has a musical ear. He screamed, transitioning excellently from*

C-major to C-minor. He has a fine purple color and a few strands of red hair. Any impressionist would die from envy at the mere sight of him. His unique range of colors obliges him to prefer Cezanne. In terms of other specifications, I will give you more details as soon as I start nursing him. As soon as can get out of bed, I will write and tell you what directions the windows face. I'm still lying down and am unable to sit up. Please send a pencil and some sugar.

I am sending you a kiss, my sweet, good, beloved husband.
Yours,
Sonya
PS I need two kopecks so I can make a call from the phone booth once I can get out of bed.

Dear Sonya,
It was wonderful to hear that he is red-headed. Through him you will be able to fulfill your passion for cats. With those extravagant colors of his we could deliver him as an abstract exhibit d'art if he doesn't behave.

I am throwing you 300 kisses. Tell me what direction the windows are facing but don't get out of bed too prematurely. I'll send you a rope ladder in my next package that you can throw down to me and I'll crawl up and kiss you.
Yours,
Osya

Dear Sonya,
How are you? Read this letter very carefully. I will deliver this letter at 11:30 a.m. You will most

likely read it before 1:00 p.m. As soon as you have read it, please answer telling me which direction the windows are facing. At 5:20 p.m. I will be standing below your windows. Send down a rope, and I will fasten a bag of books to it. I have chosen two for you. One by Strugatsky, entitled The Return. The other one is by Anatole France, four volumes of stories. If you don't think that's good enough, give me a call, I will be home between 4 and 4:30 p.m. If you feel like having a little cake, I'll send that along.
Yours,
Osya

Dear Sonya,
Here are the cookies you asked for. Sorry, I accidentally ate some of them. They taste so good. Remember to continue getting proper rest. That way you'll get discharged quicker.
Yours,
Osya

Dear Sonya,
Hurray, hurray! We now have a grandchild whose surname is Nabutovsky. First name: still unknown. Name of father: Iosif. Year of birth: 1965. Month and day: November 24. Time of birth: 4:35 a.m. My dear little Sonya, how happy I am, I am jumping for joy! Firstly, upon receiving the news that you are doing well, secondly, from hearing that the child is doing well, too, and thirdly, from hearing that the father of the child is very happy.

> *See you soon in the free world.*
> *Your mother-in-law,*
> *Vera*

As we waited for freedom, a nurse would turn up every morning. She would be carrying a mop and a pail with disinfectant. We were many women in the ward, there was also a woman in her late forties who confided in us that she had had her thirty-second abortion. She could have been telling the truth because abortions were our only means of prevention. The nurse ordered us to lie on our backs and spread our legs, whereupon she would do the rounds, disinfecting each of us with the mop. Her hands would keep a firm grip on the mop as she pushed it up and down between our legs. Each time, my heart would stop beating, full of loathing.

> *Dear parents,*
> *Our heartfelt congratulations on your newborn child. We take delight along with you on the birth of a newborn child, a new citizen of the Soviet Union and a member of the future communist society. We wish your family good health, love, and friendship. We are certain that you will bring your child up to perform conscientious work and to become a loyal patriot of our great Fatherland.*
> *The City Council of Leningrad*

Alyosha

While I was at the maternity clinic, Osya had bought a refrigerator, our very first one. It was just as fascinating to me as a space rocket. Oblong and equipped with three shelves, it was very modern and its door opened upward. It could hang on the wall and it took up no space in the small five-and-a-half-square-meter kitchen. Very convenient. "We are going to catch up to and overtake America," was the slogan back then.

The previous year, in 1964, yet another Russian "tsar," Nikita Khrushchev, had been deposed. He was the man in the Soviet Union who stopped the bloodbath from continuing, and, contrary to the mass murderer, Stalin, he wanted the best for his people, but never came to understand that there might be other opinions as to what was best. He gave the people what he thought was right for them. In the cities more apartments were built, and out in the country you were permitted to own a cow. He was the man who traveled to the United States to meet JFK, and in America he learned that happiness was to be found in endless corn fields. They had to be the solution to the constant lack of meat in the supermarkets. The more food there was for the animals, the more meat there would be for the people, and, in that way, it might be possible to produce the much sought-after sausages everyone kept dreaming about. It never dawned on Khrushchev that the problem was that the collective farms were receiving orders as to when they could plant and when they could harvest by the powers that be, who were situated far away, and with the implementation by the District Party Committee. There was absolutely no doubt in Khrushchev's mind that you could order crops to grow whenever and wherever you wanted them to.

Just like the people normally reacted to the absurdities of life with a joke, they now answered with a joking song:

> *Don't come visit me, Nikita*
> *Don't set your young girl's passion on fire,*
> *For I have eaten my fill of corn, Nikita,*
> *And you can forget everything about love and kisses.*
>
> *Refrain:*
> *Yes, we will get our bodies used to corn*
> *because without corn communism can't be built.*
> *For the corn performs, as we all know, miracles,*
> *and if there is corn then there will also be sausages.*
>
> *My lover was thinner than a finger,*
> *as skinny as a louse with tuberculosis.*
> *Then he started eating corn and got so fat*
> *that my arms could no longer reach around him.*
>
> *Refrain:*
> *Yes, we will get our bodies used to corn*
> *because without corn communism can't be built.*
> *For the corn performs, as we all know, miracles,*
> *and if there is corn then there will also be sausages.*

Now, the fields of the Soviet Union, one-sixth of the entire globe, were to be planted with corn. Also up above the polar circle. The sorely tried population was constantly being exposed to one undertaking after another, large campaigns that everyone had to partake in. With every campaign it was promised that everything, this time, would turn out well.

When the great initiatives fell flat with a crash, the disappointment was real, but after a while you grew rather callous. When the corn refused to shoot up, the nation let out a sigh of relief and Nikita was thrown out together with the corn.

I returned home from the maternity clinic. The day-to-day life with a baby began. Life continued. We still weren't allowed to see the many films we heard about. We knew that Bergman, Visconti, Kurosawa, and Fellini existed, but their films weren't shown. We still weren't allowed to read what we wanted to. No Solzhenitsyn or forbidden poets like Mandelstam and Tsvetaeva. We weren't allowed to travel outside the country, and there was continually less meat.

Nevertheless, happiness didn't loosen its grip on us. There were so many other joys. Computer science was starting to gain ground. Previously, computer science and genetics were considered to be fake science, and therefore had been forbidden research areas. They had been perceived as something corrupt and petit-bourgeois, but that view had changed, and at work Osya was deeply buried in the wonders of computer sciences, electronic calculators, while he was writing his PhD. It was back in the days when you wore white smocks when working with those machines that were later to be known as computers.

I was on maternity leave from my job at the Ethnographic Institute but continued studying Russian literature at the university, while washing diapers and devouring sci-fi novels. One of the novels was about a scientist who is on his deathbed. Some of his colleagues come over to visit him, but on the way to his house they encounter some barriers, and the closer they get to his house the more barriers they face. It turns out that all the scientific institutions of the entire planet are in the midst of entering the contents of his brain into a gigantic electronic calculator. A large area is barricaded off because the contents of his brain take up too much space. Again, this book was about a utopia. All of society would be on the right track, and storing a person's brain was a contribution to the global development. Naturally, it demanded a huge of capacity. It demanded the joint efforts of the entire planet. It was the dream of a futuristic world in which humans manage to achieve a common good by working together.

Friends would come and go from our home. We lived in an *otdel'naia* (separate) apartment, which, in contrast to a *kommunalka*, was intended for one family. My father moved in with another woman, so it was only my mother, Osya, Alyosha, and I who lived there now. We were in the fortunate situation of not even having to know our neighbors. After having lived for many years in a *kommunalka*, it was considered a luxury. Nevertheless, we were never alone. Our home was always filled with friends, a little paradise on earth. Beautiful. Cozy.

Hemingway was the trend of the time, and it was common to have his portrait standing on one's bookshelf next to a bunch of other little knickknacks. We decorated the place further with a little Georgian copper pitcher, a green ceramic bowl from Estonia, a Bulgarian cup. Across from the bookshelf there was a sofa, which unfolded to make a bed, a writing desk, and a chair. Next to that was a box with a vacuum cleaner in it, and, on top of that, our son in a big cardboard box.

The apartment was located on the edge of town. We were in the last of a row of tall concrete apartment complexes next to a large undeveloped stretch of ground. This in turn, further out, bordered on that cemetery where those who had died during the siege were buried. We lived only twenty minutes away by bus from Nevskii Prospekt, the main drag of Leningrad, and the bus stop was right next to our home. Our friends would get off there. The entrance ticket to our home was nothing other than to hand wash as much diapers as possible, this being the time before disposable paper diapers and even before washing machines. It was participatory friendships. We helped each other—that was how things were in the Soviet Union. We talked ceaselessly, read the forbidden poets, and had high-flown conversations.

I nursed my baby every fourth hour and read books on child-rearing. Dr. Spock believed that it was the parent's duty "to keep the child on the right course with firmness." When Alyosha cried and cried at night, we strung a ribbon through his pacifier, put it in his mouth, and then tied the ribbon around his head so that the pacifier wouldn't fall out. We didn't do that with any bad intentions.

After a while, we started noticing that Alyosha was pale and wasn't gaining enough weight. We took him to a policlinic. It was a brilliant concept: all medical services were concentrated in one place, so that the distance between a general practitioner and a specialist was negligible. For example, you didn't have to wait a week to get an X-ray appointment, instead, you could get it immediately and then went back to the general practitioner or to a specialist.

At first, the general practitioner couldn't find anything wrong with Alyosha, but we weren't content with that. Through some friends of ours, we got into contact with a professor of children's diseases, whom we paid to visit us at home. He believed that our son had a heart defect, which was later confirmed by the pediatric clinic. Alyosha was hospitalized in a ward where there were also children suffering from leukemia which, back then, was a fatal disease. The other mothers looked at me with envy because my Alyosha "only" had a heart defect. I felt privileged and was confident that my son was going to get well.

Every day I made the trip to the hospital where he was admitted. I walked up, left my street clothes in the cloakroom, and was given a white smock, which all visitors had to wear. I walked down the hallway, greeted the nurses, and went into the ward where my son lay together with the somewhat less fortunate children. One of them, a boy of twelve, was also named Alyosha. His mother cried constantly, and from her weeping the boy was able to decipher his fate. In the shadow of the godless society of the Soviet Union there was no comfort to be found in the belief in an afterlife. He was like any other ill child: quick to mature and equipped with a knowledge of life which very few children of his age have. Alyosha sat with my Alyosha on his lap and together we hoped that he would get better because he didn't suffer from leukemia. We had a shared interest in science fiction and talked about the immortality of the world and that we, as a part of that boundlessness, would be resurrected on a different planet. That was how things went day in and day out. But Alyosha didn't get better.

I was determined that my child was going to get well. Heart surgery was still at the experimental stage at that point, but in Moscow a lone doctor had started operating on very young infants who suffered from heart defects. The hospital in Leningrad arranged for the necessary contact with the clinic in question, and I traveled there with Alyosha. He was hospitalized but I wasn't allowed to stay with him due to hygienic reasons and was therefore denied access to the ward.

My father's older sister lived in the city. She was a stocky woman who was busy from early morning to late at night waiting on her big family. I was given lodgings with her and stayed there for the next few months. I knew very little about her because my father hardly ever mentioned his family, and we didn't get closer to one another while I was in Moscow. Her husband had been killed in the beginning of the Second World War. There was a rumor in the family that as a young man *he had known Stalin*. It was always a consolation to have just a few privileges in a society that otherwise referred to itself as classless. Those that had known some of the heroes of the revolution could easily spend the rest of their lives touring around and telling of their fleeting moments in history.

> A man comes home and finds his wife in bed with someone else. Furious, he thrusts himself upon the lover and threatens to kill him. The wife steps between them and shushes him. "Don't you dare!" she says as she points reverentially at the lover, "that man met Lenin once."

While there was much prestige in having been close to God, it didn't get you any extra square meters. The pattern from my childhood repeated itself when I came to Moscow: again, there were tons of neighbors and a shared kitchen, and, again, there were eight families sharing an apartment. My aunt lived in a big room with my cousin and her small child in addition to my other cousin, his wife, and their son of five. I was given a spot on a foldout bed behind the dining table.

There was a wall of silence surrounding all of my father's family. My aunt never started a sentence by saying "When your father was little..." to reveal a funny story about my father as a child. My grandparents were never mentioned. I don't know who they were as people, what they worked with, where they lived, when they were born, when they died. I have a single photograph of my grandfather and his two brothers. One of them, my grandfather, dark-haired with a well-groomed beard, was hardly distinguishable from Chekhov. If you don't know what Chekhov looked like, then, perhaps, you know what Harrison Ford looks like instead? Indiana Jones! My grandfather looked like Indiana Jones with a beard. The two other brothers in the picture were very fair with fine mustaches. All three of them nice-looking young men in suits and white shirts with stiff collars, my grandfather wearing a frock coat and with a cigarette dangling nonchalantly from his hand. They could have been office workers or artists, doctors, but most certainly not farmers or manual laborers. They were never mentioned in my family. What kind of cross did my family carry? Perhaps they belonged to the wrong social class? They had been adults during the revolution and had bred the new generation of loyal Party members who, in some instances, preferred that their social origin be forgotten. As in so many other Russian families, the history of my grandparents has disappeared into an impenetrable universe.

Alyosha first had to be examined and then operated on. I wasn't permitted to see my son and didn't question it for a single moment. There was a risk that I might bring infections from the outside were I to visit him. Every morning I got up early, removed my foldout bed, and left the apartment so as not to fill up space in the family's already cramped universe. The examination took time, and all I could do was wait.

When I didn't walk the streets of Moscow through and through, I would often take the tram number 17 out to VDNKh, Exhibition of Achievements of National Economy, or simply just the All-Russian Exhibition Center. Imagine an Acropolis submerged in Tivoli[1], only twenty-seven times bigger and filled with lavishly decorated pavilions constructed with a vast number of architectural nuances as a testimony to the power and progress of the Soviet Union. Spires and columns, cupolas and obelisks. A fairytale land. Like a kind of Hollywood.

The Statue of Liberty of the film industry, as portrayed by the woman holding a torch in her raised hand on Columbia Pictures' logo had, in Moscow, been replaced with a male worker and a female collective farmer bidding visitors welcome far above the entrance to VDNKh, the place that produced dreams. Evidence of technological, industrial, and agricultural achievements in all spheres—from microbiology and labor unions, as well as corn seeds and the tobacco indus-

---

1   An amusement park in Copenhagen.

try to rabbit breeding, space rockets, and atomic energy—was exhibited among loads of gilded statues, water fountains, and flower gardens. One of the pavilions was constructed as a memorial for the impressive space program, which the Soviet Union launched by way of Sputnik in the 1950s. Just outside the area, a glittering 100-meter-tall space obelisk of stainless steel stretched toward the sky, indicating the new Soviet exploits out in space. In a palace called "The Day-to-Day-Life," one could peer into the joys of the future, which would someday characterize life within the four walls of the private home. With your own eyes you could see for yourself what was in store for you: washing machines, blow dryers, and all the other wonderful electric home appliances to ease your daily life. The exhibits represented everything that the Soviet Union was striving to achieve. The pavilions looked like crystal balls in which everything appeared to be bright and hopeful.

Had I lived in a different time and in a different country, I would probably have gone into a church to pray to the higher powers to help cure my son. Religion didn't exist in my generation. The absence of God had been scientifically proven. Churches had been destroyed, shut down, or transformed into museums, businesses, warehouses, whatever. The role of the Church had come to an end, and the belief in God had been replaced with a belief in progress. Religion had promised us paradise after death—if we behaved properly, that is. Just like the Church, the Soviet Exhibit Center prophesied a gospel, the socialist gospel. The belief in progress, in communist progress, promised us the same paradise, only here on earth, which was undoubtedly the more preferable of the two.

Belief is like having a musical ear: either you have it or you don't. Is one more fortunate if you have the ability to share joy, hope, and pain with the higher powers? In my loneliness, I warmed myself in the golden light of the statues.

You couldn't help but feel happy upon seeing the Exhibition of Achievements of National Economy. We warmed ourselves under the covers of the Soviet blanket there in the midst of the Cold War. All the fear and terror from before were over and done with. A fresh new life had begun, and there were great expectations for the future. The Soviet Union had taken a step further out into space. In the course of twenty minutes, floating in an orange spacesuit next to an oblong space ship and holding a movie camera in his hand, Aleksey Leonov—the first person ever—had taken a stroll into open space. In the Soviet circus—the biggest in the world—bears would skate and become international celebrities. The Bolshoi Ballet danced beyond the country's boarders, touring in foreign countries. We Soviet citizens all floated in a new universe, a new era. We were waiting to catch up with and overtake America. We were waiting for communism to be implemented in twenty years, so that everyone could finally give according to one's ability, and receive according to one's needs.

You couldn't help but be happy. The young heart of the nation was beating in Moscow, the best city on the planet. I had arrived there with a very special mood deep down under my skin, for we had all seen *Walking the Streets of Moscow*. It was the lightest, most wonderful film you could imagine back then—and we who were young in the 1960s in the Soviet Union used to hum, for many years to come, a song from the movie:

Sometimes life can be so good and you don't immediately understand why. A light summer rain is falling...

The main character was played by the then eighteen-year-old Nikita Mikhalkov. Later in his life, Mikhalkov settled the score with Stalin's terror when he directed the movie *Burned by the Sun*, in which people disappear one by one as victims of the terror regime. Mikhalkov wasn't the son of just anybody. His father was the very poet who had written the lyrics to the national anthem of the Soviet Union:

> *Unbreakable union of freeborn republics*
> *Great Rus has united forever to stand!*
> *Long live, created by the will of the peoples,*
> *The united, the mighty Soviet Union!*

At the VDNKh, there stood sculptures of the free Soviet Republics, like Greek goddesses in gold, because the word "republic" is feminine in Russian. Wrapped in sprays emanating from the middle of the fountain, the goddesses were the very heart of the exhibit, fifteen statues standing in a circle around the golden sheaf in the fountain, symbolizing the common effort, two thousand streams under pressure. But we, the next generation, took a step down from mythology toward the more ordinary and mundane life. We went from the solemn patriotic songs to those that were more intimate and quiet and that did not inspire heroic deeds. It was like going from "Hail to the Chief..." to "Yesterday... all my troubles seemed so far away..."

It was spring, and I was strolling around at the exhibit. We were young, there was nothing to be afraid of. Our child was going to get well. Everything was going to be okay...

Sometimes life can be so good and you don't immediately understand why. A light summer rain is falling. The usual summer rain.

Alyosha got the flu, and the operation had to be postponed. He was sent to another hospital where he received treatment. This time I was allowed to be with him a few hours each day, so I would take the trolley out to the hospital, past the zoo and the long wall leading to the notorious Butyrka Prison. I spent the days with Alyosha and watched him get better and better. My little boy smiled at me, and all was good.

> Telegram
> March 30, 1966
> I, Sofia Nazarovna Nabutovskaya, 9 Klyuchevaya Street, apartment 12, Leningrad K-221, grant the power of attorney to Iosif Nabutovsky so that he can receive my pay from the Ethnographic Institute at the Scientific Academy of the USSR in Leningrad. Stamped at the Fifth Public Notary's Office in Moscow. A government fee of 50 kopecks has been paid.

My dearest sweetheart,
I went to your work place to deliver the power of attorney, but the bookkeeper was in the bank, so I had to leave without having achieved anything. Afterward I went to the university with your written excuse for absence. But the office there was closed. I am sending twenty rubles. I don't have that much money, but if you would like to buy a pair of summer shoes, I will send you more. I'll call you on Tuesday at around 11 a.m. I have an exam tomorrow. Say hi to everyone for me. If Edik buys a ticket for the soccer match on the 29th, then tell him to buy a ticket for me, too. Kisses from Osya.

May 30, 1966
Dear Osya,
I have good news: the result of Alyosha's blood tests are much better than last time. His hemoglobin is 72 now as opposed to 62, which it was

> *before; the sedimentation rate 9 compared to 28 before. He will most likely be moved back to the Clinic on Monday. I'm doing well. Say hi to the family for me.*
> *Kisses from Sonya*

Alyosha was operated on shortly afterward and died during the operation. Once again, I was denied access to the Clinic for hygienic reasons, but could pick him up at the mortuary. I sat waiting for a long time in some car or other before going in.

Osya was there, too. He must have been. I don't remember. Why is it that you can't share grief?

"You can go in now and dress the baby, little mother," a woman said to me when I entered the mortuary. Alyosha's body lay on a metal table. Cut open all the way down through his sternum and sewed up again with big stitches. A cold and wet little body. I asked for a towel so that I could dry him and put on him the new clothes which I had bought in Moscow while I was waiting for him to get better. I lifted him up to place him on my shoulder, and a reddish-brown liquid spilled from his mouth and down my clothes.

Planernaya, outside of Moscow, a barren and empty space, with a newly built cemetery close to what was earlier a runway for gliders. The soil was dry, and I remember thinking it was a good thing that he wasn't going to be buried in Leningrad because the soil was so moist there. The casket wasn't closed until the coffin was to be lowered into the ground. I had some small daisies with me and put them down, down on his clothes, which by now had reddish-brown stains on them. I tried to cover them. A male voice warned me that one doesn't place flowers in a coffin. "They are to lay on the grave," he said. I got irritated. No one was to tell me where I should or shouldn't place the flowers I had brought for my son.

But what had they done to my child? A little body cut in half and no explanation was all I had left.

That same evening Osya and I traveled with the night train home to Leningrad. He left for work early the next morning. I ate breakfast alone, took a tram to the hospital where Alyosha had been hospitalized before he was moved to Moscow, fell asleep in the tram, woke up at my stop, entered the hospital, left my clothes in the cloakroom, was given a white smock. I walked up to the old ward down the hallway. A nurse greeted me warmly and asked me about my stay in Moscow, as two other nurses showed up, curious to hear how things had gone with Alyosha. At that very moment I suddenly woke up. I had forgotten that I had been to Moscow. That my child was dead. I had just automatically got up that morning and gone to see my son. I was twenty-one years old.

Kaliningrad

In 1966, the legendary football player Franz Beckenbauer, "Der Kaiser," played his first soccer world championship. The Soviet Union was competing for the gold medal, but lost 1–2 to Germany in the semifinal round. It was "Der Kaiser" who scored Germany's second goal.

I heard the match as I strolled around the streets of Kaliningrad together with Osya. It was hot. The sun was baking down on the depopulated scenery. The inhabitants sat watching the match, glued in front of their TVs, and through the open windows we could hear the cheerful roar from the crowds, Beckenbauer's name, and the disappointed voices that echoed off the gables in the empty streets. In the meantime, we played the role of tourists. We were on vacation. Osya's cousin had tempted us with the beach and the ocean.

I had been in Kaliningrad before, in my early childhood. It had been one of the several postings to which my father had been assigned when, like most men in the Soviet Union at that time, he served in the military. Leningrad, Tallinn, Rostock, Kaliningrad, Leningrad.

First stop: Tallinn. I was born there by accident.

The Second World War was in its final stages. In Estonia, the battered population had lived behind a bloody backdrop for years. The country was taken over by the Soviet Union right before the beginning of the War. The new regime immediately arrested and executed thousands who, as they believed, might put up a resistance, and deported thousands of others to Siberia. Then things quieted down. The thunder of the totalitarian state resounded all over Estonia. Afterwards, the

Germans came and installed a new reign of terror, and at the end of the War the Soviet army returned to the Estonian battlefield and chased the Germans out. Nothing really changed, except for the executioners and the victims who always change according to whoever happens to be the ruling party. The population remains the same.

My parents' home was Leningrad, where my mother had lived during the War. When the army reached Tallinn, she, heavily pregnant, ventured forth on a short journey with the night train to visit my father. The plan was that she would return to Leningrad to give birth to me, as the army would set out on its victory march through Europe. But things didn't turn out that way. Apparently, I loved my father so much already while in my mother's womb that I wanted him by my side as soon as I came out into the world. As a result, Tallinn became the one spot in the world with which I was never to have anything to do later in my life, but to which I nevertheless feel a certain connection solely due to the fact that I was born there.

I was the child of a liberator—or an occupier—all depending on how you look at it. And I was one of the children who had to make up for the Soviet Union's great population loss during the War. We were the country that had suffered the most casualties: eleven million soldiers and sixteen million civilians. Twenty-seven million people.

I got a birth certificate which stated, in Russian and in Estonian, that I was Jewish. And then we moved on—continuing the victory march together into Germany with the army that was trembling with sorrow and a thirst for revenge.

We arrived in Rostock and were put up in a house by the Baltic Sea. My mother, who, contrary to the Germans' plans, hadn't died from famine and managed to survive the siege of Leningrad, got a job and had to employ a nanny. Bertha was German. I don't remember her. She exists in my consciousness prior to my memory. Everything I know about Bertha I know from my mother. Bertha is a mythical figure from my childhood, the good fairy that stood by my cradle. She was my first great love, that woman who had her own quiet way of opposing world history.

"How did you manage to communicate with Bertha?" I once asked my mother because Bertha only spoke German. My mother explained that she didn't have much choice but to summon bits and pieces of the Yiddish she knew from her childhood, and, somewhere between the meeting of those two kindred languages, she and Bertha found a common understanding and perhaps a shared sense of humor. In any event, one of the family stories from my childhood is from a day when Bertha was out walking with me and we were stopped by a German who patted my head of blond curly hair and called me "ein echtes deutsches Kind," a real German child.

The repercussions of the War resounded throughout Europe. My father was transferred to Kaliningrad. Known as Königsberg, that city had been a large German cultural center, but the War had demolished it. The German people had been forcibly removed, and all that had been left was a shell of a city, the ruins of which had been given a new name after Mikhail Kalinin, the Soviet Union's head of state.

"What?" you ask. "The Soviet Union's head of state? But that was Stalin!"

No. He served as the Secretary General of the Communist Party. He was the generalissimo, the general above all generals. Mikhail Kalinin was the de jure head of state, a conflict-averse figurehead who legitimized Stalin's killing machine. He was the one who signed all the death sentences. He was the one who signed the resolution stating that all Soviet citizens could be shot without having a trial, including children from the age of twelve. He was the one to whom millions of Gulag prisoners appealed to no avail. His own wife was also arrested and sent to a work camp. She was imprisoned there, while he was the Chairman of the Presidium of the Supreme Council. He died just after the War, and so the city was named after him.

Königsberg. Kaliningrad. The city got new inhabitants that came from other ruins around the Soviet Union. The Navy set up its headquarters there, and the city was off limits to the West. No one could or was permitted to look inside the next forty-five years. Like a stray dog, it had lost its sense of direction and wandered about at the periphery of a fatigued Russia.

That is where my first memories derive from. Little bits and pieces of memories. A tree in the garden, a barrel filled with rain water, the sand on the beach near Kaliningrad. Waves. Light. Sounds. "*Ostorozhno, osoka!*" a voice says. "Watch out!" My hand is stretched out, my fingers about to grasp a blade of grass. "It is sedge. You can cut your hands on it so that they bleed."

It is through more or less dramatic experiences throughout your life that you really gain some knowledge about yourself. Either you are satisfied with the result, or you make do. You go through life without being conscious of big chunks of your childhood, but suddenly some light is cast on a single moment that has been submerged in the dark for many years. You recall something about yourself from your early childhood, from back when you were someone else.

A living picture. A *tableau vivant*, which was a favorite party game amongst the bourgeoisie in the nineteenth century. A group of people would dress up, strike a pose, and pretend to be someone else entirely different from who they were. You would think of a historic event or a scene from Greek mythology, create a scenography, sew costumes for your family and friends. Uncle Valdemar was dressed up as a Greek god, aunt

Olga as a fleeing nymph, cousin Constantin was Cupid with a bow and arrow, and the children were animals in the forest. You would strike a pose like you would for a painting. And then what? Nothing. It was all internal. You met yourself as somebody else.

There are moments in one's early childhood that aren't left in the darkness but remain clear in the light. They resemble a first-time experience, regardless of whether it is so or not. That is all totally immaterial. The important thing is that they feel that way. It is that light that falls on them and has done so from the very first time.

Fear and Trembling

The German people were gone. They had been replaced. We live in their houses with their furniture. As the conquerors, we have the right to live in their lives, in their abandoned domain. We share a house with another family. Each family has its own room. A door leads from our room to a terrace, where piles of plates and faded German newspapers are stacked up. This door has to stay locked. "You are not to open it for anybody," I have been told. I am a small child and alone in our room. It is cold and raining. I suddenly catch sight of him. I can see him through the window panes of the terrace door. He is a foreign boy because he is wearing short pants and a jacket, and Russian boys don't wear short pants. His legs are bare. He comes jogging through the garden. He comes closer, up the stairs to the terrace, and over to the door. He grabs hold of it. It is locked. He leans forward, peers through the small window pane, directly into my eyes. I see his gaze. I can still see it now, seventy years later. He turns around and runs away.

Expectation and Disappointment

I crawl up a tree where I can easily sit between two low branches and look out at the street. I wait with anticipation. I have been told that a young girl has died of a broken heart, and before long I am going to have the chance to see what such a heart looks like. Soon a funeral procession is going to pass our house—a truck with an open coffin. The heart is in the coffin—torn to pieces, as it is said in Russian when you have got a heart attack. Far in the distance I can hear an orchestra that is drearily leading the procession, and I am trying to imagine what the heart looks like. The truck is getting closer. I am in a perfect position and can look directly down into the coffin. But there is no torn heart to be seen. Only a woman. I become horribly disappointed. Everything is so utterly dull.

Enthusiasm and Sorrow

The neighbor's daughter has a large book. Blue and thick. I can't even lift it. The pages are divided by the most delicate silk paper that you aren't allowed to touch but can blow on to make the colorful picture on the next page appear. Slowly, the paper falls back down into place. The neighbor's daughter teaches me how to read. It's as though everything falls into place, and one day I'm able to read. From that moment, everything changes, including my life. Everything else becomes secondary for me. I don't understand half the words, but that's completely irrelevant. Even though it is incomprehensible, I hear the melody of the poem. It turns out that I am sitting with Pushkin's fairytales in my hands, Russia's great poet, the embodiment of the Russian soul. From then on, I live in the world of books and remember my books better than I do my parents. My whole life becomes reading. An escape from reality.

A child's heavy burden is to obey adults. And I was born into a system based on total obedience. As a result, others are in charge of me. Life in my country is congealed into a fixed, unbreakable framework, everything is stiff and predetermined, but I don't realize that yet. The books are an escape from the prison of my childhood, the first step on the road to freedom, to being a free bird.

I am sick with scarlet fever and get hospitalized. But I have a book by Pushkin with me. Inside, there is a poem about Ruslan and Ludmila, which I read over and over. When I get discharged, the first tragedy of my life occurs. I am not allowed to remove the book from the isolation ward and have to leave it at the hospital. But the poem remains with me nevertheless. I know it by heart.

> *There's a green oak-tree by the shores*
> *Of the blue bay; on a gold chain,*
> *The cat, learned in the fable stories,*
> *Walks round the tree in ceaseless strain:*
> *Moves to the right—a song it groans,*
> *Moves to the left—it tells a tale.*
>
> *There're marvels there: the wood-spite roams,*
> *Midst branches shines the mermaids' tail;*
> *There are the strangest creatures' traces*
> *On the mysterious paths and moors;*
> *There stands a hut on hen's legs, hairless,*
> *Without windows and doors;*
> *There visions fill a vale and forest;*
> *There, at a dawn, come waves, the coldest,*
> *On the deserted sandy shore,*

And thirty knights, in armors shone,
Come out the clear waves in a colon,
And their sea-tutor—them before;

(Alexander Pushkin: Ruslan and Ludmila,
translated by Yevgeny Bonver)

We trod kilometer after kilometer along the beach, Osya and me, with the ruins of Kaliningrad as our gloomy backdrop. It wasn't until now that I really saw them properly, these twenty-year-old ruins. Like rotten teeth, they stuck out in the landscape and got mixed up with my memories.

My mother was with us because she was handicapped and couldn't stay home alone on her own. We rented a room in a house for her and put up a tent for ourselves on a slope high up above the beach with a view of the water. A fantastic place with white sand that stretched to eternity. There were hardly any people because the area was an off-limits zone and very few people could, therefore, obtain permission to travel there. We managed to get permission because Osya's cousin lived at a military base close by and had sent us an invitation. The place was very foreign looking. It was so orderly compared to the city. If you went out to the countryside in Russia, a forest was a forest, and a house was a farmhouse. But in this Russia a forest was a park with laid-out paths.

Osya and I were supposed to sleep together in the tent, but, as time passed, I was sleeping more and more together with my mother in the room we had rented for her. One morning I went down to the tent and couldn't find him. I ran around and looked for him and was very worried. I searched in all the places where I thought he could be. Finally I caught sight of him when I looked down across the beach. He was lying ever so peacefully in the sand with his science books. I shouted at the top of my lungs that I had looked for him everywhere. And that he was a rascal, I heard myself scream...

There was nothing more that could be done. Osya and I could have long and very civilized conversations about world literature, but the one thing we couldn't talk about was the death of Alyosha.

The Scent of the Taiga

I was living my life on the edge, living an intense life where everything was discombobulated, including my relationship with Osya. We lived side by side but not together. Osya went to work every day at the Research Institute for Direct Current, totally absorbed in his computers, those colossal blocks of the brave new world. The monstrosities of the West, the beauties of depravity, they were now permitted and were spread across several cubic meters at the Institute, served by brainy men in white coats. The most important word in his conscience was algorithm.

I myself had exhausted the strongest of my emotions. I was drained after Alyosha's death, and merely felt a quiet form of friendliness and sympathy for my surroundings. I felt sorry for my mother who was so young and so ill. I felt sorry for Osya whom I couldn't love. I felt sorry for my father who had a guilty conscience when it came to me because he had abandoned his sick wife and was always trying to justify his actions when we were together.

At the same time that I felt sorry for all my loved ones, I was writing articles for the newspaper *Leningradskaia Pravda*—*The Truth from Leningrad*—and was studying at the university. The degree was granted through correspondence, and there were exams every six months. I also moon-lighted as a music teacher at a kindergarten. I rehearsed songs with the children about little rabbits, kittens, and "Grandfather Lenin," and how wonderful it was living in the Soviet Union where one was loved by one's country. I would go from the newspaper office to the kindergarten carrying a bicycle chain in my handbag, which I would take with me late in the evening to the Actor's Club.

The participants there all had a job of some kind at some point during the day, but at night we would together rehearse the play *Sailors without a Sea*, which couldn't be performed at an official theater due to censorship. Instead, we would perform the play for one another. I was responsible for the music, and played with the bicycle chain placed across the strings of the club's piano in order to create a new sound. It was all terribly modern.

In addition, I would transcribe forbidden poems. It was very hard to keep people from reading. You would just take five sheets of thin paper, place tracing paper between them, and copy the most beautiful Russian poems written by poets who had been exiled, executed, or died in a Soviet camp. Very few people owned a typewriter, but my aunt in Vilnius had given me one. Aside from the fact that it provided me with a means of income—I copy-typed articles and dissertations and in that way got to know a lot of interesting people—it also led to my "criminal career." Copying forbidden literature could has cost me seven years' imprisonment.

Seven years! They couldn't put us all in jail, could they? And what would you do if you got arrested? What would a woman do if she landed in such a place? When she gets her period? How would she wash herself? Get ahold of some cotton? There are so many ways women can be degraded. Remember, we knew nothing about maxi pads or tampons. We didn't have them yet, and we used cotton, which was very difficult to get ahold of. How on earth can you start a revolution without cotton?

When it came to the KGB, you never knew what were rumors and what was the truth. They said that all typewriters were registered with the KGB. But how could you resist the temptation to write Samizdat[1]? All the wonderful things that existed but hadn't been made public were forbidden.

---

1   Self publication.

Or were they? It was like stepping into the Brothers Strugatsky's gray zone, as they described it in the sci-fi novel *Roadside Picnic*, a zone which it is forbidden to enter because an alien spaceship landed on Earth and took off again and those who were onboard left their trash. Some of the residuals are very useful to earthlings, others are invisible and dangerous if you get into contact with them. Deep in the zone, the aliens have also left a golden ball that can fulfill your deepest wishes. Of course, everyone wants to find the ball—there are a few stalkers (pathfinders) who know the route to it, but it is forbidden to travel there, and, if you do, you risk losing your life.

In Soviet reality we were all on our way to the golden ball without knowing where the border between that which was "forbidden" and that which was "permitted" was located. We had to figure out how to navigate through the zone unscathed without touching all the things that were dangerous and, at the same time, to extract maximum advantage of the possibilities that were to be found there.

We would often meet up at Stalina's room, where we gathered to sing the "self-made" songs of the time. The room was really a hallway. In a corner there was an open oven—our own little bonfire—and alongside the wall a couch with a table in front of it. A bear hide covered the small piece of floor that remained available, and a single shelf adorned one of the walls. People would bring firewood instead of cakes (which was a regular custom), and at some point a tape recorder appeared on the shelf. The hallway was part of a *kommunalka* apartment, which meant that there were many neighbors. Stalina's family had two additional rooms, which were located between the neighbors and us as a no man's land. No one crossed the boundary, and we could listen to our songs in peace.

However, some problems arose with the neighbors across from us. In order to enter Stalina's hallway, you had to pass through a courtyard surrounded by windows through which it was possible to keep track of who came and went. The neighbors from the courtyard noticed that a suspiciously large number of men tended to go in and out of the apartment. The neighbors across from us approached the office in charge of the building, which also housed a Party organization and a "comrade" court of justice—an institution that exercised legal authority whenever the communist ideology began to retreat from people's consciousness in favor of other intentions. Stalina was brought to trial and accused of impropriety. Many of the men showed up to testify that that wasn't true at all. "But what are you doing there, then?" the neighbors asked. "We're just singing," they answered honestly.

Meanwhile, out in the world, the Vietnam War was being fought.

We. Who were we? Most of the others were ten or fifteen years older than me, a generation of young men and women, some of them named after prestigious figures. It was very common for children born in the 1920s and 1930s to get names like Vladlen and Lenina—after Vladimir Lenin; Marlen, after Marx and Lenin; Rem, meaning Revolution Engels Marx; Kim, an abbreviation of Kommunisticheskii Internatsional Molodiozhi, the Young Communist International. The crowd that came to Stalina's was a colorful one. Poets and engineers, architects and geologists, the generation whose parents and grandparents had been sent to the Gulag, they were all hoping for change. I was a student and not hoping for anything. I was just enjoying life. Absorbing the atmosphere.

The building where Stalina lived was on Liteyny Prospekt, an important street in my life. It was one of the main roads of the city, with the KGB building at one end and a café at the other. The café was known as Saigon, and we would often meet there. Joseph Brodsky lived a stone's throw away. Shostakovich had as a young man written music for a theater further down the road. I had learned to play the piano in the music school across from there. And the Liteyny Bridge that crossed the Neva River and led to the KGB building was the first electrically illuminated bridge in the world.

All the horrible things that had happened under Stalin had been a mistake, we were told. One half of the country had methodically killed the other half, and no one knew how many lives had been lost. The horrible thing was that no one had been punished. There were no war crime tribunals. It wasn't written about in the newspapers, and not a word was mentioned on the radio. Everything just remained silent. The shock was simply too great. The control of the country continued as though nothing had taken place. And an army of overseers decided what was to be expressed and how.

It was as though the country had a stroke, become paralyzed, and lost the ability to speak. You weren't allowed to say the truth about the War, about the Gulag. You were not allowed to say: "We live in a police state." You weren't allowed to say: "We had been persecuted. You weren't allowed to say: "We were sent to concentration camps." What you were allowed to say was that the War had been great, glorious, and heroic. You *had* to say that.

And suddenly, in the midst of this oblivion, a man picks up a guitar and quietly begins to sing: "Oh, terrible war, what have you done?" Those words awakened the mute country and proved that it was possible to treat a patient who had lost the ability to speak by getting him to sing. That which he hadn't been able to utter out loud until now, he could sing along with instead. The "self-made songs" were curing people and giving them a voice.

> The phenomenon of "do-it-yourself songs," also known as "self-made songs" emerged in the late 1950s in contrast to the official "Soviet song," which was a genre within totalitarian art, created by those composers, poets, and singers whom the state had approved. If the song had not been granted the official authorization in the form of the Soviet stamp of censorship, if the words and the music hadn't been approved, it couldn't be played on the radio, broadcast on TV, performed in theaters, published in books, or used in films. The "Soviet song" was under total governmental control.

The unofficial self-made songs spread like wildfire thanks to the new-fangled invention, the tape recorder. We always met at Stalina's where we would sit in front of the "bonfire" and sing along with the songs that poured forth from the recorder. We put ourselves in the same shoes as the released prisoners and completely identified with those who had spent twenty years in a work camp. But the songs did not initiate any kind of revolution, because our generation was also paralyzed by fear.

Oh, the clouds go by, floating by,
Like in films they float, soft and slow;
I'm chewing chicken (spiced and fried),
And my brandy's running low.

Floating clouds sail off to the east,
Soft and slow they float, soft and slow;
I bet that they're warm as toast,
But me, I've been chilled to the bone!

Once I froze like iron to ice,
Digging roads with a pick in my hand!

I left twenty long years of my life
Back in those bloody labor camps.

I can see that frozen snow crust,
Hear the cursing when we were frisked . . .
Hey waiter!—pineapple chunks,
And another double of this!

Rolling clouds go by, sailing far
To that dear old home in the east,
They don't know what an amnesty's for,
They don't need any lawyer to plead.

Now I'm living a life without care,
Twenty years flew straight past like a dream;
Here I sit like a lord in this bar,
And I've even got a few teeth!

Clouds roll by to the morning sun,
With no pension, no trouble or strife;
As for me, well, twice a month,
I collect what's mine by right.

And on those two days, just like me,
Half this country sits in the bars!
And the clouds roll by to the east,
Rolling by in all of our hearts . . .

And those clouds roll by to the east,
Rolling by in all of our hearts . . .

(Clouds, by Alexander Galich, translated by Gerald Stanton Smith, Ann Arbor)

Every conceivable and inconceivable song that would never be accepted by the authorities emerged at that time. It wasn't just the past that we would sing about. Numerous of the "self-made" songs expressed hope, a longing, a lack of something, dreams, and it was a very specific profession that was associated with these songs: geology. There was a romanticized image of geologists because they would go on expeditions for four to five months at a time where they would explore unknown areas of the Soviet Union. They would travel out to the deserts, the mountains, stay in the middle of the taiga and far off behind the Polar Circle. They became one with the extremes. Which implicitly meant that they were outside the reach of the authorities, far away from the stifling grip of society. There were not always Party secretaries on those expeditions, but always a guitar or two. When they weren't digging for uranium or gold, the geologists would sit around a campfire and sing. After being out in extreme weather for months at a time they would always return with new songs that could be added to the already existing repertoire. When referred to someone as a "geologist," in reality we meant a person who had achieved individual freedom.

> *You can see, it's not normal, far from normal,*
> *I admit that I'm a bit of a wacko.*
> *I am chasing, I am chasing foggy mornings,*
> *And there's nothing I can do about it.*
> *Folks are busy chasing fortunes, chasing people*
> *To escape from their resentment and from woes.*
> *But I'm busy chasing the fog, busy chasing rainbows,*
> *chasing rainbows and the wild scent of the taiga.*
>
> (Song by Yuri Kukin)

I arrived at Stalina's wearing high heels, a fake fur coat, and a white mohair scarf. I looked like a beaver. The coat reached just below my knees, had three-quarter-length sleeves, and was home-made with an unusually long zipper that was broken and could therefore only be zipped halfway down. In order to take off the coat, I had to let it fall nonchalantly to the ground and step out of it. When I had to put it on again, it was the same procedure. I would take one step into it, lift it from the ground, pull it up around my body, slip my arms into the sleeves, and zip it up like you would a space suit.

My light mohair scarf had cost me twenty-four rubles, which was an insanely large amount of money for a scarf back then. My mother's pension was thirty rubles a month. It wasn't just any kind of scarf; it was knitted with a long fuzzy nap, which was terribly modern and considered one of three status symbols. The other two were leather jackets and toned eyeglasses. Both the scarf and the mohair yarn were in themselves completely unobtainable in the Soviet Union unless you were acquainted with sailors or ballet dancers who were some of the privileged few permitted to travel abroad. They would often return with a load of mohair scarves, the colors of which were typically harsh. Mine, on the other hand, was cream-colored. Beautiful. Soft. Delicate.

It was the month of March, but winter hadn't yet loosened its grip on the city. I had gingerly walked through a snow-covered Leningrad, and now I let the fur coat fall to my feet in Stalina's hallway and tossed the scarf across a chair. Stalina's brother, who was a geologist, and his friends had just returned from several months of temporary freedom, and the smell of taiga blended with the warmth from the oven. We were all sitting there around the bonfire, including Joseph Brodsky. His red hair lit up in the room as we gathered, tightly packed, around his penetrating voice. Like waves hitting a shore, he recited his poetry.

Brodsky was the celebrity of my generation. I was there on the wings of history. I am able to puff myself up and take off from the ground because I have been in the same room as him and because he left the room with my scarf. Those in power used to call him a "parasite," because in the Soviet Union you had to have a job that was beneficial to society, and whatever that was entailed decided by the government. If you didn't have such a job, you were considered a criminal—and a poet who wasn't approved of by the state was definitely a criminal. Brodsky didn't have an official job and wrote poems without being a member of the Authors' Guild. So, he was arrested and had to stand trial.

> Judge: And what is your general occupation?
> Brodsky: I am a poet and literary translator.
> Judge: Who has acknowledged you as a poet? Who has included you in the ranks of the poets?
> Brodsky: No one. Who has included me in the ranks of humanity?
> J: Have you studied to do this?
> B: To do what?
> J: To become a poet. Haven't you applied to a school of higher education where you learn such things?
> B: I wasn't aware one could learn such things.
> J: How else could you learn it?
> B: I think it comes from . . . God.

(Excerpt from Joseph Brodsky's trial)

Brodsky should never have said that. He was exiled to a small town outside of Arkhangelsk up by the White Sea. However, he wasn't exiled because he believed in God. He claimed that he earned a living from writing poetry. If that were true, then, according to the rules, he should have been a member of the Authors' Guild, which he wasn't. That was his crime, and he was punished for it. The system was unmerciful toward those who stood out. You couldn't deviate one step to the left or one step to the right; you could only walk along the established Soviet path.

That night at Stalina's Brodsky left after having read his poems aloud and took my scarf with him. I saw him take it from the chair but didn't say anything. I was much too flattered over the fact that a legend would want anything that was mine. I crawled back into the spacesuit and left together with two of the young men who had been present that evening—two geologists. They had been away from the pleasures of the big city for such a long a time. I slept with both of them. It was pure charity on my part; the scarf for Brodsky, my body for the geologists. I lay there like a plaice, without thinking, without feeling anything. Afterwards, I got up and went home.

I staggered through the snow drifts in my high heels to the streetcar. At the tram stop, the window pane of a kiosk was plastered with the morning papers. There was a big picture of Gagarin on the front pages. I took a closer look. The picture was framed in black. Gagarin, together with his flying instructor, had been on a routine practice flight the previous day, and the small plane in which they had been flying had crashed. The country had lost its last hero.

Back at home, I said to my husband that it was time we get a divorce. He had known it would happen, he said, but it had to come from me. Osya packed his bags and went home to his parents. When he left, I started to cry. I sobbed and sobbed even though I knew it was the only right thing to do. We were so young and our marriage couldn't withstand the loss of a child.

Sausages with Stewed Cabbage

I was living together with a foreigner, which was strictly forbidden in the Soviet Union. Foreigners were only allowed to reside in hotels and, in rare cases, student dorms but under no circumstances in the flats of Soviet citizens. That was the easiest way for the authorities to keep an eye on them. My foreigner, my Ole, had gone back to Denmark during the Christmas break, and I wanted to surprise him with a candlelight dinner when he returned to his forbidden home. I wanted to prepare a meal that had literary reminiscences, a dish that was taken from Mikhail Bulgakov's novel *The Master and Margarita*.

When you have a favorite book, it retains much of its life in quotations. My copy of *The Master and Margarita* was in shreds after having been read ad nauseum. Not just by me, but my entire generation. It was our book. The inhabitants of the godless country were shaken because the novel described the suffering of Jesus and Satan's visit, in person, to Soviet Moscow.

"The Devil lifted the lid of the saucepan. It revealed little sausages in tomato sauce." I wanted to make a sausage dish in which I would add all my passion, my longing—and stewed cabbage. My dinner was to manifest itself like a culinary blend of love and triumph.

Triumph, because sausages were equivalent to mayonnaise and green peas, which is to say, extremely difficult to obtain. It wasn't because there wasn't enough food in the shops—it was because they didn't have anything that you'd actually want to eat. There were pyramids of canned fish and chocolates that didn't contain much chocolate. But on rare occasions there was buckwheat and, on even rarer occasions, sausages. You didn't purchase them, you "managed to get ahold of" them because no one knew which shops had them in stock or when they would appear. Life could fluctuate from minor to major depending, on whether there were sausages the day you happened to be standing in line, or buckwheat, or another thing that was hard to get. At some work places you could buy packages with the coveted sausages, but you would be forced to include other items in your purchase, items which weren't quite as sought after, if not downright unwanted. A half a kilo sausages might mean four jars of ready-made cabbage soup being added to your purchase. It says a great deal about the Soviet Union that, when the country disintegrated, the appearance of Danish hot dog stands on the city streets announced the start of a new life.

I lived in a country that both produced and distributed according to planned economy. First, I called the closest grocery store but was given a clear "No" to my question as to whether they might have some sausages. There was no luck at the next store I called either. Then I called a third one where they asked if I was crazy. Of course there were no sausages to be had anywhere!

Whereupon I seriously got to work on it and called the district's head of distribution who referred me to someone "higher up." I kept at it, got ahold of the individual in question, and gave him a long sob story about how I was going to have the exceptionally rare opportunity of receiving foreign guests in my home. I had promised those guests, who were all experts in Russian literature, to prepare a dish from *The Master and Margarita*—as they were all extremely well read. I insisted that I couldn't possibly let my guests down and simply had to get ahold of those sausages. Finally, there was a breakthrough. At long last, I was informed where I could find those damn sausages.

It was, of course, on the other end of town. But they were the most wonderful sausages I had ever seen, delicious-looking and pink with a light purple nuance like the neck of a dove. I got them delivered in the office by the shop's female boss, carefully packed in brown paper so that no one could see what I was carrying when I left the office and walked through the shop. There was, of course, another way of obtaining sausages, namely, if you knew someone who knew someone who knew someone who dealt with sausages. My connections were clearly lacking in the sausage department.

My beloved Ole returned to the USSR and was served sausages with steamed cabbage and tomato sauce, though he didn't express any particular enthusiasm for the dish. I had executed a military operation as if it had been a matter of life and death in order to get those sausages, but I don't think it ever entirely dawned on him. On the other hand, he was happy to see me and had brought presents with him. Soap, "Imperial," which was my first aroma from abroad. Pantyhose, the first in my life, which were equally as coveted as sausages and buckwheat. *Abbey Road*, my first Beatles record ever. Outside on the road, he had parked the black Volkswagen, which he had driven all the way from Denmark. It was the only Volkswagen in all of Leningrad and, therefore, it drew a lot of attention. The KGB was also parked outside on the road.

My very first encounter with Ole occurred when I was going to an exam at the Leningrad State University. In front of the door to the exam room stood a group of foreign girls and a single man. They looked different, had a completely different scent, and struck me as fantastically beautiful. I asked where they came from. "Denmark," one of them said, to which I cried, "How exotic," because everything non-Russian was extremely exotic. I wasn't thinking of palm trees, coconuts, or azure oceans but of something uncommon. Something that usually only appeared in fairytales. We spoke with one another briefly before I was called into the exam room, and they were still standing there when I came out.

They were students from the Slavic Institute in Copenhagen, and they were on a nine-month scholarship. This was their first day in Leningrad, actually their first day in the Soviet Union in general, and they had a million questions. Before we parted ways, I gave them my telephone number, just in case. They had to remember to call me *not* from the student dorm but from a telephone booth. A few days later I received a phone call from the only man in the group, Ole Vesterholt. He asked whether I would be interested in coming to their housewarming party at the student dorm where they lived.

I showed up for a short time because I already had another engagement for that evening—and ended up sitting next to Ole. I remember that he very gallantly wanted to light my cigarette and struck a match. My hands were trembling slightly, as they always did. When he held the match towards me, I noticed that his hands also trembled. We hadn't yet said a word to each other. Our first contact had been a look into each other's eyes and a good laugh over the fact that our hands were trembling.

The student dorm room where the party took place was tiny, with two beds adjacent to one another. The only thing separating them was a small chest of drawers. This is where we sat, a bunch of students seated on the beds by a small dining table. More and more guests arrived, and chairs were gradually fetched from the other rooms and the common kitchen. We had a wonderful time in those few square meters.

On the wall across from me there hung a photo. In one of its corners, a small piece of glass had been broken off the frame. Inside the picture, I could see some small specks of fly droppings. "Well, it's not exactly a portrait of Emperor Ferdinand," I exclaimed when I caught sight of it. "No," Ole responded concurrently, "the flies got there before the innkeeper did."

For most people those two comments are probably incomprehensible, so let me explain. Ole and I came from two different worlds but one thing we had in common was that we both had read the Czech classic book *The Good Soldier Schweik*. And we both recalled that Schweik frequented an inn where the innkeeper had removed the portrait of Emperor Ferdinand and placed it in the attic so that the flies wouldn't leave their droppings on him. What were the odds that Ole and I would meet and find one another in the joy of a shared recognition? That our paths would intersect at the hearth of literature? There was a huge distance between the closed Soviet Union and Denmark. The distance was huge between our backgrounds, upbringing, and experiences. But the distance disappeared when we met in *The Good Soldier Schweik*.

> Love leaped up out at us like a murderer jumping out of a dark alley. It shocked us both—the shock of a stroke of lightning, the shock of a switchblade knife...

(From *The Master and Margarita*)

Discussions, drinks, cigarettes, titles, names, and quotations. It continued endlessly. But I had to move on that night. I went down to the street to hail a taxi—even though I was a student, I could still afford taxis and champagne. They were cheap items in the Soviet Union. Ole followed me and did something which I was later to discover was completely out of character for him. Ole a very reserved person was through and through, but at that moment he realized I was about to disappear from his life just as swiftly as I had entered it. "Now, I don't want you to think I'm crazy," he said as I waited for a taxi to show up, "but I believe you are the woman in my life, the woman whom I am going to marry." We had known each other for a few hours when he declared his love for me. At that very moment a taxi came. I put forth my hand and said, laughingly, "Maybe you should sleep on that." And then I was gone.

The next day I was standing on a landing at the university when Ole came running toward me. "I HAVE slept on it now!" he shouted, "I HAVE slept on it now!" It dawned on me then that the man actually meant what he had said the night before. At that very moment, I was struck by fate. The next sixteen years of my life began at that moment. Ole and I couldn't tear ourselves apart from one another. We couldn't bear being apart, even though Ole shared his dorm room with another student. In the following weeks, his toothbrush was the first thing that disappeared from the dorm room, then ever so discreetly his shirts, and finally the rest was put in a suitcase. Ole moved in with me, and the forbidden home was now a reality.

The other Danish students lived at the dorm. And they were monitored. The security guard at the entrance knew precisely when they left and came back. They had to be careful when they took a taxi to their new Soviet friends. In the USSR you could get into deep water if you had had any contact with a foreigner, so the Danes had to make sure they got dropped off close to the address and also that the taxi was out of sight when they made their way to their destination. And, of course, "Uncle Vanya" was listening in on their conversations. The KGB had their "eyes and ears" in every floor of the student dorm. Nevertheless, I was convinced that the foreign students did not take the monster seriously and did not fear it like the rest of us. That as long as they had their foreign passports they could avoid a blow from its tail.

Ole, a linguistic genius, had studied Serbian and Czech. Russian was the last station on his journey through the Slavic languages. The year before we met he had been in Prague for a couple of months and experienced the 1968 Czech Spring uprising at close proximity. He had witnessed the attempt to introduce socialism with a human face and how that face had been crushed by Soviet tanks. Back home in Denmark he had participated in a Danish television program in which the event had been thoroughly analyzed and discussed, and it was most likely at that point that the KGB began to notice him. The USSR was afraid of the Czechoslovakian germ that might begin to spread and contaminate others.

There wasn't a shadow of a doubt. From the first night we met each other, Ole and I were destined to be together. But, in order for that to happen, we would have to marry. There was only one place in Leningrad where you could marry a foreigner: at the Wedding Palace by the Neva River. You had to apply for it a month in advance, but we were afraid of sending in the application because it might lead to unpleasantries for both of us. All the information would in a matter of no time end up in the hands of the KGB, and if the powers that be didn't approve of our marriage they could prematurely order Ole out of the country or ruin our plans in some other way. As a result, we decided to take the typical Russian approach—take a detour.

My father had been previously married, and my wonderful half-sister had a job at a distribution center from where books were sent to book stores. Books were considered hard currency in the city, an extremely coveted commodity, and especially those books that were published in modest numbers. The walls of the book stores in Leningrad were covered from floor to ceiling with books, but, just like with food items, there was a huge gap between that which the people wanted to read and what the government allowed them to read. One of the most sought-after books, otherwise known as "the little black volume" amongst connoisseurs, contained "The Trial" and other works by Kafka. That book was worth its weight in gold. My wonderful, helpful half-sister went to the Wedding Palace in order to speak with the manager with whom she was already acquainted. Would it be possible to make an exception in this particular case? The impossible suddenly became very possible with Kafka on the table! The manager had no problem finding a wedding date and circumventing the registration period.

However, it was necessary to obtain one specific document. We had to approach the Danish Embassy and get a written statement that Ole was not already married. The problem was that the embassy was located in Moscow, and we were in Leningrad, and all our phone lines would, of course, be bugged. Ole had to hop on the Red Arrow, the night train to Moscow, in order to speak with someone at the Danish Embassy. There he was told that it would take a week or two to obtain the necessary paperwork, whereupon he returned to Leningrad with the first night train.

There was always an excuse to celebrate something or other in the Soviet Union. Astronauts, women, the Soviet Army, the fishermen, the military, the fiftieth anniversary of the implementation of the first Unpaid-Labor Saturday (Subbotnik). Life was a party... so, while we were waiting for the important document, the entire nation was celebrating Lenin's 100th birthday. The festivities reached hysterical heights. They conducted as though it was the "end of history." It was clear that the history of man was developing vertically upward: from the dawn of humanity to the stone age, slave societies, feudalism, capitalism, socialism, and in communism we finally hit the ceiling. The abyss between reality and the propaganda universe of the powers that be immediately inspired jokes amongst the people.

> In honor of Lenin's anniversary a number of Soviet companies manufactured some new products. A furniture manufacturer developed a three-person bed called "Lenin is always with us." A perfumery developed a soap "for the places Lenin has visited."[1] A clock-and-watch factory developed a cuckoo clock from which, at noon, a figure of Lenin with an extended hand[2] would come forward and say "cuckoo, comrades, cuckoo."

A few weeks later, Ole once again got on the Red Arrow to Moscow and returned after thirty-six hours with the document in his hand. The following day we were informed of the wedding date.

We had no money. My "capitalist" wasn't a rich Westerner, and we had to constantly count our pennies. In order to be able to afford the wedding, Ole decided to sell his suede jacket, which would bring us a nice amount of money. It was considered a criminal act, but it was necessary. Without informing me of the plan, he set out for the market one morning and returned beaming with joy. He had made a good bargain—and threw two thick bundles of paper bills on the table. Fortune had smiled upon us, until we discovered that he had been grossly cheated. The top and bottom bills in both bundles were genuine, but everything between them was newspaper sheets.

Notwithstanding all the obstacles, it was a beautiful May morning in 1970. Our wedding day. Spring had signaled its arrival in April when the ice began to melt on the Neva River. Now ice floes drifted through the city—they originated from

---

1 An allusion to a popular attraction in the Soviet Union—trips to places associated with Lenin's life and career.
2 An allusion to the popular image of Lenin raising his right hand. Monuments of Lenin were usually made that way.

the Ladoga Lake up north, reminding all of Leningrad that summer was now just around the corner. In the morning, I sat in our little kitchen cutting the threads hanging from Ole's worn jeans which he was going to wear. I had borrowed a knitted pink mini-dress from my best friend who was shorter than me by a head. It was going to be a stand-up wedding because it was technically impossible to sit down in the dress. If I did, it would crawl up below my breasts, that's how short it was. But terribly fashionable.

Ole and I left the apartment separately—just to be on the safe side—and arrived by public transport to the Wedding Palace. We were the first ones who were married that day, not in the princely ballroom where the ceremony usually took place, but in an office on the ground floor. We were husband and wife, and no one had managed to create any obstacles for us in the process.

When we arrived home there was a suspicious looking car parked on the street, but we didn't care. My mother and our friends were waiting for us up in the apartment with champagne we had bought. We had not thought about serving food except for a Napoleon cake, which we had baked under my mother's expert supervision.

Suddenly the doorbell rang. We exchanged frightened glances. Outside there stood a concerned neighbor with tears in her eyes. Her puppy had eaten a cloth and she couldn't get through to the central exchange to order a taxi so she could get to the veterinary hospital. Could we perhaps help her? The party was immediately postponed as we raced down to the Volkswagen with a semi-choked puppy lying in the arms of the sobbing woman. The car that had been parked outside our door followed us as we headed toward the vet.

Meanwhile, the guests had chipped in to buy some food. When we returned, still with the now easily recognizable car on our tail, the table was set with herring, potatoes, sauerkraut, and pickles. The already familiar car was parked further down the street and its engine was turned off.

What is happiness? It could be the lack of unhappiness, it could be the warmth of a puppy, it could be when you are understood. With Ole I felt understood. He understood the happiness and unhappiness of the Soviet people, the absurdity of our socialist life. He had the ability to forgive, to be happy together with us, and share in our joys.

That evening, after the guests had gone home and Ole had collapsed from consuming too much alcohol, I sat alone in the kitchen with a book when the doorbell rang. Again, I got a scare. It was the neighbor again. But this time she was happy. She thanked us for our help. The puppy had now managed to defecate the cloth out.

Ole's visa expired shortly after the wedding. He applied to get it extended, but his application was denied and he had to return home to Denmark. The one who remained in the USSR was Sofia Vesterholt, the official spouse of a Danish citizen.

Roadside Picnic

While Ole was still studying at Leningrad University and we weren't married yet, he went back to Denmark for the Christmas break and returned after New Year's. Before, I could have convinced myself that my boyfriend wasn't a Westerner, that he came from one of the Baltic states, Estonia, for example, because he was tall, blond, and handsome, which were typical features of Estonians. But now it became evident that he was from the West through and through.

Ole drove into Leningrad in his father's Volkswagen. A shiny and cute black bubble. Not only was it an unseen and unheard-of phenomenon, it was also a wild and impermissible luxury. There were no auto dealers in the USSR. They simply didn't exist. Who was allowed to own a car, and who wasn't, depended on one's workplace. Some selected places were granted a certain number of cars every so often. You could apply to be signed up for one of the cars, but you had to deserve to get into the line. It was an advantage if you were an active member of the Party, a good worker, or an informer. It was a broad field. You had a number of options. The applications were discussed at the Union or Party meetings, where the decisions were also made. The successful applicants would get a permission to purchase a Moskvich or a Zaporozhets, two locally made models. There were no other possibilities for ordinary people. And for ordinary people it meant having to shell out a three- or four-year salary when they finally got the coveted vehicle. Had it been my mother, for example, she would have had to cough up the equivalent of a ten-year pension.

Of course there were other cars to be seen in the city. Many high-ranking officials with chauffeurs drove around in Volgas, the Soviet equivalent of a Mercedes. And then there was the Chayka, which means "seagull," the Cadillac of the Soviet Union. In the Chayka, the members of the Political Bureau would whizz by, far above the rest of us.

> After a prolonged selection process, a man is informed by his employer that he has been selected to be the lucky owner of a Moskvich. "When can I get it?" the man asks excitedly. "On December 13, in ten years, " the employer answers. "Excuse me," the man asks carefully, "but could you tell me whether it will be in the morning or afternoon?" His employer gives him a perplexed look. "Why do you need to know?" he asks. "What difference does it make, as long as you get the car?" The man gives him a serious look and says, "It's just that the plumber is scheduled to come in the morning."

"Imagine winning a car," I could lie and dream out loud when I was fifteen or sixteen years old, as I lay in my foldaway bed on one side of the piano as my mother lay on the other. She couldn't see me, but she listened to my daydreams. They didn't deal with travels to exotic beaches with palm trees and the sound of rippling waves but with being able to afford food and clothes—and some relief from having to take care of my mother, although that was a dream I kept to myself. My mother was paralyzed, my father was away a lot of the time, in the process of leaving her. I was fifteen and had just stopped going to school. I eked out a living by playing the piano and writing on my typewriter. "Imagine winning a car in a lottery, then you could sell the lucky ticket to a rich Georgian for a whole lot of money." The dreams reached all the way to the top of the ceiling above our twelve square meters. In the quiet night, the most beautiful city in the world sent a white glow through the thin curtains, lighting up the room. In the white nights of Leningrad, you could see the dreams standing in line.

Aelita's bedroom momentarily gave way to the wealthy Georgian. How could one ever become so rich as to pay the excessive prices for all the things that were hard to obtain? In the Soviet Union we had an idea that people from Georgia possessed a lot of money. While it was cold at our latitude, it was warm down south in Georgia, which gave them the advantage of being able to cultivate mandarins. We children got them in our goody bags for New Year's, two mandarines that smelled fantastic. Mandarins and flowers were the Georgian gold mine. They could be sold at the markets in the Soviet Union and bring in a fortune.

I could see the suitcases before me, in which the mimosas and the mandarines were exchanged for thousands of rubles. The Georgians could barely drag the money with them when they made their way back home. It would be easy, I explained to my mother as we settled down to sleep, to find a rich Georgian who would buy my car which I had won with the lottery ticket I hadn't yet bought because there were many people who wanted to obtain a car without having to wait in line.

I lay looking up at our curtains with the lilac flowers, they figuratively adorned the room with fragrance—as I made numerous plans. How could I win a car? How much could I get for it? What and how much should we buy with all the money? I multiplied and divided, added and subtracted. Finally, my mother said, "May I please sleep a little now, honey? You can just keep calculating."

When foreigners visited Leningrad, they weren't allowed to stay privately with anyone. That was why the only two places in town where you could admire foreign cars—from a proper distance, of course—were the Hotel Europa and the Hotel Astoria. However, it should be said that Eastern Europeans fell slightly outside of that category. They were lower in the ranks, stayed at Hotel Moscow, and never arrived by car.

And now there emerged an entirely new, a third possibility to see a foreign car: at our concrete paradise on Klyuchevaya Street in the outskirts of town. The very different-looking elegant Bubble shone at the bottom of the otherwise anonymous block of buildings. The Bubble shone clearly, and it was also clear to everyone that a foreigner resided there. We displayed ourselves for everyone and everything. We exposed ourselves completely. Why wasn't the foreigner staying at Europa or Astoria? Why was he living with a Soviet woman? The whole thing was extremely suspicious, so there was a good reason why a car was often parked further down the road with two men who would set off in pursuit of us every time we drove off in the Bubble.

All foreigners, without exception, were under observation. All contact with foreign countries, whatever form it took, was considered suspicious. Woe to the one who might be tempted to reveal the totalitarian state's stinking secrets to the West, or, as the authorities called it: be responsible for leaking negative information regarding the USSR to the outside world.

It was winter when Ole drove into Leningrad, and the Bubble immediately fainted from the cold weather. We tried to take various engine parts up with us to the apartment during the night. Maybe they could come back to life if they lay snug under a warm blanket. For example, Ole discovered that the battery was in much better shape the next day after having slept on the bathroom floor.

The Bubble wasn't always so cooperative. Several times, it downright refused to start, in which case it would be parked down below our window as Ole tried unsuccessfully to get it going. But thank God for the fact that we were under observation! The two men further down the street who were getting paid to follow our every move could sense when a fellow motorist was in distress. Didn't they feel a longing deep within their guts when they could observe our troubles from their surveillance post? Didn't their fingers itch to come over and help Ole in order to behold this extraordinary specimen at close proximity, touch this rarity? Or did they only want to insert the key in the ignition and speed after the Bubble through the city? Prove me wrong if those two especially selected for the job weren't struck by an adventurous sense of joy when, on a clear and frosty morning, I came running over to them and said, "Okay, comrades, if you don't help us push we'll never get anywhere." All I know is that they jumped out of the car ready to come to the rescue, helped us, and thereupon followed us as usual.

The Bubble became a work-horse in Leningrad because with it we were able to help our wide circle of friends. We would fetch and transport them, drove mothers-in-law around town and lovers to their rendezvous, furniture was transported on the roof of the car, and empty bottles delivered to the grocery store in order to contribute a little to the housekeeping money. Imagine if Roman Abramovich, one of the richest men in the world, came sailing on his yacht, lowered his anchor at Costco and walked in with a couple of bags of empty bottles. That was the effect the Bubble had on the people of Leningrad in 1970. Their jaws dropped when they saw us arrive with the luggage compartment full of returnable bottles and nudged us forward if we got in a long line. In their eyes we were much too refined to have to live hand-to-mouth like that.

But the Bubble was also a problem, because, no matter where we drove, the people we came into contact with became visible to the KGB. Once we wanted to take the car over to my cousin's but he made a big to-do about it when we called to say we were coming over to visit him. Over his dead body! He was employed at an optic research center and was therefore not allowed to communicate with foreigners. We had all heard the story about his colleague who had been laid off because he had danced with a foreigner while on a business trip in the Far East. The fear sprung forth in my cousin when he with his mind's eye envisioned the monster's tail flicking dangerously. The eternally latent fear, which had crept under our skin generations ago, deep into our blood stream, and was now an ingrained part of the Soviet people's DNA. What kind of secrets did the powers that be think he could leak to us? That Brezhnev perhaps used +5.00 strength in his glasses? I never got a chance to see my cousin again, and he died before the Soviet Union fell apart.

One day, for the umpteenth time, the Bubble wouldn't start. No matter what we pulled out of the hat, it just wouldn't budge. Not even the KGB could help us. It had to go to the mechanics', where all the workers eagerly gathered around it. They had never seen a Volkswagen before. If we came back a few days later, they would be able to tell us what was wrong with it, they said. When we returned, the Bubble had been completely disassembled. (If you could send a spaceship into outer space then you could most probably also disassemble and reassemble a Volkswagen.) All the engine parts had been removed, meticulously numbered, and placed on a table. It appeared that the engine was broken and a specific part needed to be replaced. That specific replacement part was not available anywhere in the Soviet Union, which was vast, but apparently not vast enough. But it could be found in Finland.

The coveted object was just 400 kilometers away, but the question was how were we going to get ahold of it. Ole couldn't pick it up because, if he left the USSR, he wouldn't be allowed back and would therefore have to travel back to Denmark and apply for a new visa. Neither I nor any other Soviet citizen was allowed to travel to Finland to pick up the replacement part because we weren't permitted to travel abroad, regardless of whether it was a capitalist or a socialist country.

However, should you entertain a wish to travel abroad, which clearly went against all regulations, the Party Committee at your work place would have to take up the case, consider the pros and cons, and declare you either worthy or unworthy of the trip. If you were so miraculously fortunate as to be declared worthy of the trip, the case would be passed on to the District Party Committee, and the next step would consist of a personal interview. You would appear before a panel that would determine the extent to which you were prepared to encounter foreigners. The interview was more like an exam than a dialogue. Afterward, the final verdict would be announced. I myself knew a man who had been denied permission to travel because he was unable to tell how many members there were in the Communist Party of Nicaragua!

If you, for some odd reason, happened to have access to such knowledge, you could dig out your Russian-English phrase book from 1962 and start preparing to have interesting conversations with exciting foreigners. There were common ordinary phrases like "Where is the lavatory?," "What does it cost?," and the more intrusive "Are you a member of the Space Committee?" Furthermore, according to the phrase book, Soviet tourists, who always traveled in groups, had an irresistible urge to break out in spontaneous declarations:

> Excerpt from a phrase book
>
> The friendship between the Soviet and the English peoples makes us glad.
> Please extend our congratulations to the hero of the day.
> We're for peaceful coexistence.
> We are striving to have the highest living standard in the world.
> We learn communism in labor and struggle.
> The first artificial satellite of the Earth was launched by the Soviet Union on October 4, 1957.
> We are conquering the outer space in the name of science and progress.
> Please take this "Soviet Rocket on the Moon" badge.
> Let's trade!

Ole went to the Finnish consulate—the only place in Leningrad that represented the West—and explained the situation, that he wasn't able to obtain the spare part. Fortunately, they agreed to help but advised that it would take some time. We prepared to wait patiently.

Even though the Bubble had disappeared from the city scene, we were still under observation. My relationship with a Dane was apparently dangerous for the population of one-sixth of the globe, but that didn't bother Ole. Like most foreigners, he didn't have fear in his blood. The whole thing struck him as rather absurd, but for ordinary Soviet citizens it was extremely serious business. Our society was supposed to be a paradise, but those who resided in that society lived in hell. When they tried to survive, they were punished for not pretending that they were living in paradise.

I was just as frightened as everyone else—afraid of the unknown—like a small child who is afraid of entering a dark room because the monster is under the bed, flicking with its tail as it waits for the child to step closer. But I knew that the monster didn't exist only in the child's fantasy. It was for real, regardless of the fact that at that time the murders had come to a halt.

The adrenalin ran through my body and the fear was transformed into a fighting spirit. I asked myself, "What can those assholes threaten me with?" I had already experienced the ultimate pain in life. My son was dead and I had buried him. So what in the world did they think they could threaten me with? KGB's little tricks were peanuts in the bigger scheme of things, practically a fairytale that merely made one feel more significant.

Finally, a courier arrived with the awaited spare part. All of the car's numbered vital organs were reassembled, and the replacement part was screwed on. We went to the mechanic to pick up the car. Ole had a bottle of whiskey under his arm, which he had bought in a currency exchange shop; I came with a selection of cakes and a couple of bottles of Baikal, the Soviet equivalent of Coke, because we had some celebrating to do. The Bubble looked radiant, the corks popped, and the workshop supervisor made a speech about the brotherhood of nations. Toasts were made for Denmark and the Soviet Union. We were surrounded by warmth, admiration, and understanding. The triumph was total. The car started without any problems, of course, and we drove back to the apartment complex. The next morning a car with two men was once again parked further down the road.

We were married in May and made a bold decision. We wanted to see if the Bubble could manage taking us on a honeymoon trip to Moscow. A quick trip consisting of 650 kilometers each way. It was beautiful out in the countryside, it was spring, and there were dandelions as far as the eye could see, pine and spruce trees towered above an untrimmed idyll in the never-ending countryside that reached the moon. And we most surely resembled creatures from another planet as we came driving there in the Bubble, moving through the landscape along the asphalt road, every so often passing a control post with a couple of uniformed traffic officers.

Every so often we noticed a dirt road or gravel road leading away from the main road and into the forest, where a moose in its sole majesty might stretch its neck and let out a cry that disappeared across the treetops to never reach our ears. We parked the Bubble by the wayside where we sprawled out with the picnic basket we had brought. Surrounding the fields and meadows were large forests, and in the middle of the forests there were deep lakes. Yes, it was most certainly gorgeous out there in the countryside.

In the distance, the sound of a motorcycle could be heard as it came closer. It slowed down when it was quite a way from the Bubble and finally stopped when it was directly behind us. A police officer dismounted the motorbike and asked in a friendly, but firm, tone where we had disappeared to. Disappeared to? . . . But of course! It goes without saying that it wasn't every day that you encountered visitors from another planet! For a brief moment, under the influence of the beautiful scenery, we had forgotten that there were eyes following us all the way from Leningrad to Moscow.

One of the traffic control posts reported: "A foreign vehicle has just passed. Heading in your direction. Copy?" "Roger that." When the Bubble had torn past the next post, it would report us to the next one, and the next one, until a couple of officers suddenly sat looking in anticipation for the small creature—all in vain. In their view, we had simply disappeared into thin air.

Out in the humongous Russian countryside where the birds chirped and love blossomed. We hadn't "disappeared" but had sat down at the wayside with our picnic basket. That was all we had done. We hadn't driven off some country road to reveal the great secrets of a collective farm.

The black Volkswagen had received so much attention in the Soviet Union, as it never saw before and would never receive again. Males tended to gather around it, men and boys who wanted to have long conversations with Ole about the car, help get it started when it wouldn't, admire it, disassemble and reassemble it, and so on. It became a little celebrity and had its brief heyday in Leningrad. After that, it returned to Denmark where it led an obscure life until it was decommissioned and hauled off to the scrap yard.

The Last Summer

We are in a sparse concrete room, there are no windows. Two men are sitting at a table in the middle of the room. At a distance from the table, on the opposite side of it, is a chair. I, Shitty Couch, am sitting in that chair, my hands and feet tied with a rope. A single lamp in the room sends its sharp light directly into my face so that I can't see the two men. Ominous music fades in.

Really? No, no, it's only in the movies that those kinds of things happen. The terror wasn't nearly as visually expressive in the Soviet Union at that time. It was, on the other hand, a battle of words, and the concrete room was a completely nondescript office.

One of the men throws a jab to the right: "Your mother is sick. You have applied for permission to travel abroad. How can you possibly abandon her?"

I duck: "That's no problem, I'll figure it out."

They throw another jab: "Oh, but we can help you when you arrive in Denmark."

I attempt a block: "No, thank you. I don't care for your kind of organizations, Gestapo, KGB and such."

They punch me in the kidneys: "How dare you compare us with the Gestapo? Just be grateful this isn't 1937."[1]

That really hit me in the gut. I understood that had it been then this conversation would have been of a very different kind. In 1937 the terror was at its peak and the methods very different. A conversation back then consisted of torture

---

1 1937–1938 – Years of Great Terror in the Soviet Union

and executions. I grimace and move in close to stifle the blows. Yes, but we *aren't* in 1937 and thank heavens for that!

The first round is over and we each retreat to our respective corners of the ring.

Seen from the KGB's point of view, they were facing a person whom they had to convince to cooperate with them. That was clear to me. However, what exactly did this cooperation entail and what was it they really wanted? And what methods would they use to make you work with them? They always start with intimidation even before it is clear how you could be useful to them, but the fear must always be there at the very start.

We returned to the ring.

"Does your husband realize how many men you've known before him?"

The sexual dagger is the KGB's favorite weapon. They catch people in compromised situations to blackmail them afterward.

I throw them an uppercut: "My husband, Ole Vesterholt, comes, as you know, from Denmark, which happens to be one of the first countries to experience a sexual revolution right now. You are very welcome to inform him of my earlier experiences. He would only be proud of me."

"Your husband is residing with you. That is illegal."

I continue blocking: "He has done so the last nine months with your car parked outside like a watchdog."

They attempt a KO: "Sunday, the 13th of January, you were together with your husband in a military area. What were you doing there?"

They gave me a piece of paper and asked me to write down an explanation. I began:

> My former husband, Iosif Borisovich Nabutovsky, 23/59 Kronverkskaya Street, apartment 78; my good friend and hus-

band-to-be, Ole Christian Vesterholt, 25 Vester Street, Tåstrup, Denmark, enrolled at Leningrad's State University, University Dorm, 5 Shevchenko Street, room 25, residing with Sofia Lazarevna Drissen, 9 Klyuchevaya Street, apartment 12; and I, Sofia Lazarevna Drissen, 9 Klyuchevaya Street, apartment 12, were in a car model VAZ-2101 that belongs to my former husband, Iosif Borisovich Nabutovsky, 23/59 Kronverkskaya Street, apartment 78, and were out skiing on Sunday, January 13, 1970, upon the invitation of Iosif Borisovich Nabutovsky, 23/59 Kronverkskaya Street, apartment 78. My then friend and future husband, Ole Christian Vesterholt, 25 Vester Street, Tåstrup, Denmark, enrolled at Leningrad's State University, University Dorm, 5 Shevchenko Street, room 25, residing with Sofia Lazarevna Drissen, 9 Klyuchevaya Street, apartment 12, and I, Sofia Lazarevna Drissen, 9 Klyuchevaya Street, apartment 12, had accepted the invitation. My then friend and future husband, Ole Christian Vesterholt, 25 Vester Street, Tåstrup, Denmark, enrolled at Leningrad's State University, University Dorm, 5 Shevchenko Street, room 25, residing with Sofia Lazarevna Drissen, 9 Klyuchevaya Street, apartment 12, was very pleased to get the opportunity to do some skiing.

Since my cursive handwriting tends to be rather large, those lines filled the first two pages of the explanation. I giggled every now and then as I wrote very meticulously in the most beautiful handwriting I could muster. The two men sat with their arms crossed as they waited.

Being kept under surveillance by the KGB is like being on LSD. It's a psychedelic experience. There are these constant patterns surrounding you. Leningrad was surrounded by control posts, and the Soviet Union was surrounded by enemies, and when the patterns were broken an alarm would go off in the KGB offices. One Sunday morning that winter I got into a car with some friends to drive outside of the city to go skiing. Before we even got that far, we were stopped by the militia and ordered to turn around. There were very few cities in the Soviet Union which foreigners were allowed to enter, and even they were surrounded by a restrictive radius of several kilometers. It turned out that, without even knowing it, we had been on the verge of entering forbidden territory.

I continued writing my explanation regarding our innocent motivations, listing everyone's names and addresses. When I asked for another sheet of paper, they grew impatient. They could see the absurdity of the situation. Both they and I knew that it was utterly irrelevant where we had been with our skis on that sunny winter's day or why. This was about something else. They took the papers from my hands. I was admonished not to tell anyone where I had been and they let me know in so many words that they intended to bring me in again. This was just the beginning and I still didn't know what they wanted with me. For the moment, the bout was left undecided.

During all the time that Ole and I lived together in Leningrad we were most probably always under surveillance, sometimes more visibly than others. After we got married, he had to return to Denmark because he couldn't get his residency visa extended. We talked on the phone together and wrote each other letters but were well aware of the fact that the phone calls were being bugged and the letters opened and read.

At one point, a French military ship, *Normandie*, arrived in Leningrad on a friendship visit. They sailed directly into the closed-off world on a sunny day. François, an interpreter whom I had met when he was studying Russian in Leningrad, was part of the delegation. He called and invited me to see the flagship. I saw a fantastic opportunity.

At a distance, all of the city's inhabitants crowded behind the barricades to catch a glimpse of the foreign war ship. Under the blue summer sky, François and I, however, walked through a large contingent of militia, KGB agents, and monitors dressed in civilian clothes who were standing inside the barricade. Through a fence of glances. François was wearing a snazzy French navy uniform and showed his pass as I stood triumphantly by his side. They couldn't touch me in front of all those people. And there, on French territory, outside of the grip of the KGB, I seized the opportunity and wrote a long letter to Ole in Denmark, in which I told him everything that was happening in my life.

François introduced me to some French navy officers, whom I invited over for a visit at my home. I had the place to myself, my mother was in the countryside, and I felt like I had a whole palace at my disposal. It was an immensely proud hostess who invited them inside the two-room apartment. And they were extremely enthusiastic because, had it not been for my invitation, they wouldn't have had the opportunity to visit a private Russian home. No one else dared invite them, but I had nothing to lose. We drove in three vehicles to Klyuchevaya Street: two taxis for us and a KGB vehicle as an escort.

When we arrived at the apartment, the two taxis drove off while the KGB vehicle remained parked just outside. Looking back on it now, many years later, I can't help thinking about how different we were. What did the Frenchmen in their light-colored uniforms get out of coming to a block composed of concrete buildings in the outskirts of town? I was so poor back then, yet I was so happy and proud to host them. In my own home. There was no food in the house, so I invented a very exclusive drink right there on the spot: "White Nights," which I managed to convince them was the latest rave in Leningrad. You take boiling water, add a pinch of vanilla-flavored sugar and a drop of lemon juice. And voila. I served it in beautiful porcelain, for effect. The Frenchmen sipped the drink enthusiastically with their pinkies extended.

We spent a long evening under the glow of the white nights discussing Molière, Balzac, and Zola. It was mid-summer, and all the windows were open. A field with blossoming flowers bordered the block of concrete buildings. We chattered away, while Francois had the unenviable task of interpreting our conversation all night. The KGB men took turns sleeping in the car outside. The white nights aren't white. They have a tinge of alternating pastels. The night was pink, sweet-scented, and wonderful.

In the middle of the night, we once again called for some taxis and the Frenchmen returned to the harbor. My soul was at peace because Ole would receive my letter about how things were going. The KGB car left too. They knew that I was alone at home now. I called Osya and asked him to come immediately. He drove me to the main train station and lent me money for a ticket. I took the next train heading south and disappeared from the city.

Back then, the Soviet national anthem began with the words, "Unbreakable union of freeborn republics / Great Rus has united forever to stand." Later on, the lyrics were changed because it turned out to be a lie. The republics weren't free. The union wasn't unbreakable. They were not united for all eternity. The only true words in the song were "Great Rus." Another song was also used when great patriotic feelings were to be expressed: "Wide is my motherland, with her many forests, fields, and rivers! I know of no other such country where a man can breathe so freely." Any kind of propaganda always contains a grain of truth. You attach the lie to something everyone agrees on. And in both instances we agreed that our country had endless boundaries—with many forests, fields, and rivers. The rest wasn't true.

> The music, on the other hand, never lies. Both songs begin with a perfect fourth. A perfect fourth is an interval. An interval is a jump, or the distance, between two notes. Try singing two notes from the Battle Hymn of the Republic. "Glory Glory Hallelujah! Glory Glory Hallelujah! The notes corresponding to "ry" and "ha" are separated by a perfect fourth.

In Western culture, the perfect fourth is always referred to as something grand. We have to move onward, perform something heroic in such an interval. Just like the start of the *Internationale*, the *Marseillaise* and *Hail Grenada*. I felt like a hero when I stepped aboard the train, humming to the "Wide is my motherland."

Just like an interval between two notes, intervals may arise in life. Spending some days in a train, traveling a couple of thousand kilometers, is a solace for the soul. It feels like recess time in school. There is nothing you can do in that time, and you can't do anything about it. You are just being pulled along. I was on my way to my last summer at home in the Soviet Union.

The expression "to find your niche" has a literal meaning in the Russian trains that travel for long distances. You settle down in your niche, your bunk, where you sleep and where you might stay for one, two, three—up to seven—days, all depending on how far you had to travel.

Life on the train starts with everybody receiving their bed clothes. The men change into sweatsuits, and the women to smocks in which they can loll about. People bring provisions for several days. Hard-boiled eggs, meatballs, pickles, bread, and boiled chicken, wrapped in newspapers, salt in small match boxes. Tea and water can be purchased on the train. When four people in a compartment unwrap their food, they can't help but begin talking with one another. And sharing. A good part of the trip consists in consuming food. A sense of mutual belonging is created.

We had a sense of being at home. "My address is neither a house nor a street. My address is the Soviet Union," were the lyrics to another song. The private space on the train was almost nonexistent, and was therefore quickly transgressed within the first hours of the voyage. We lived in a common room. We flowed into each other.

After a few days of traveling by train, I arrived in the Crimea, the vacation paradise of the whole country. This peninsula by the Black Sea had a magnetic effect on the gigantic Soviet Union. Every single pot was taken up. It was like living in a *kommunalka* apartment, only this was voluntary. During the summer, house owners and their families would move into a small barn, and every nook, cranny, and bed would be rented out to the pale northerners. I had rented such a bed. In a room together with some other people. You were only indoors when you had to sleep, anyway.

I got a sunburn already on the first day. Down south the night comes abruptly. I glowed in the dark and howled from pain. All the others immediately called for a crisis meeting. What were they to do with me? One ran out to buy creme fraiche, in which I was to be smeared in order to cool down the burn. Another went into the kitchen to make tea. Complete strangers immediately dealt with the situation. There I was, Shitty Couch, sitting in the center of the room, smeared in creme fraiche and covered by a sheet. The host's dog came by and licked my toes in sympathy. I was sunburnt but happy.

On the one hand, I experienced joy from being in my country, my home, with "my family." On the other hand, a sense of sadness. It was a very common thing to exchange telephone numbers and addresses with people you met from Moscow, Vladivostok, Novosibirsk. But now, whatever new acquaintances and friendships I made wouldn't continue because I was in the process of leaving it all. Leaving my first life.

If I was granted permission to travel, would I be allowed to return to the Soviet Union? And if so, when? If I wasn't allowed to travel, what would they do with me? And when would I be able to see Ole again? No matter what happened, things were going to be very different.

My trip to the Crimea was a trek through the south with my small suitcase in my hand and a view of the soft, green Caucasus Mountains. I walked on the country roads wearing my Danish summer dress which Ole had sent to me. Already there was a touch of the West about me. In the same package there had also been a pair of shoes, white with blue polka dots, that matched the summer dress and one piece of the scent of freedom: a bar of soap. Cars would stop and pick me up. I stayed over at strangers' houses in the summer country.

Everything was peaceful. There was nothing to be afraid of. Totalitarianism can also have such a face. I would sit in the small Soviet kitchens until late at night, reciting poetry and drinking myself into a stupor with the representatives of the State Sanitary Control at the collective farms where they cultivated grapes. At the same time, I missed Ole terribly. It felt like a physical pain, not being able to share this light summer feast with him.

In Yalta I rented a room with a family where the husband worked in the city's administration. One day he said that I had to leave the town immediately. He would help me get an airplane ticket since they were difficult to obtain during the peak season. I asked why I had to leave so quickly. What was going on? At first he didn't want to tell me, but, finally, after demanding a very solemn promise that I wouldn't tell a soul—he informed me that a case of the cholera had been detected in the town and they feared it might turn into an epidemic. There was a plan to lock down the town the following day and isolate it from the rest of the country, so people who were on vacation wouldn't be able to go back home and spread the infection.

The vacation was over. Wearing my Danish summer dress, with the scent of Danish soap trailing after me, I traveled home to take up the battle against the KGB from whom I had fled after the Frenchmen's visit. Fear was always a large component of my life. The all-too-familiar nausea-inducing anxiety popped forth once again, completely overwhelming me. I wasn't so brave when it came down to it. Far, far from it. I had to learn to defeat my fear. Find a way to stand up to the KGB. And that way was to be found in most unusual method—a birthing technique.

When I, at twenty, gave birth to my son, prenatal classes were completely unheard of. So you had to find a way of enduring the pain on your own. A kind soul gave me some good advice back then. She explained that a contraction doesn't last forever, only a few seconds, and it is, therefore, easier to endure the pain if you count the seconds. That way you know that it will end at some point.

I started counting inwardly to myself: 1–2–3–4... Fear makes you dizzy, and fear makes you nauseous. I could transform the dizziness and nausea into a physical pain or ache in my stomach. That pain was much easier for me to deal with. It would just disappear after a while. There is a huge difference between having fear and having a stomachache. I taught myself to use that method in fearful situations.

I returned from my escape sun-tanned, well-dressed, and full of expectations for the future. Within five minutes upon entering my home in Leningrad, the telephone rang.

"Sofia Lazarevna?" the voice said on the other end. I started laughing. Someone in the building had apparently been given orders to inform the KGB of my return. I was proud of the fact that they hadn't managed to find me while I was traveling around down south. But the vacation was now over. They called me back in again.

I dream that I enter a room. In the room my mother stands naked on all fours on a table. I am familiar with this nakedness. I have washed her so many times in my life. Her breasts, her head, her hair that is hanging down her back. She is drenched in sweat. Her body is glistening with the sweat of pain. She is rocking back and forth. She is surrounded by people wearing white smocks. I don't know whether they are doctors or the ones who are causing her pain. She lifts her head and sees me entering the room. She smiles through the pain and says, "Moi shchenochek, my little puppy." Her love is like a physical wave of warmth, a ray, coming toward me from the violence of pain. She rises above the torture. She is in a different dimension. It is the greatest physical manifestation of her love for me I have ever experienced in my life. They can't harm us.

Once again, I refused to cooperate with them. Two days later, my application to travel to Denmark was denied on the grounds that my mother was ill and a guardian would have to be assigned to her. I went to a lawyer and got a copy of the paragraph of the laws dealing with the appointment of a guardian. My mother's case did not fall under that category. I asked to have a word with the head of the visa department and brought the letter of rejection and the copy of the paragraph. "The rejection I have been given is illegal," I said, "I'm going to complain to the highest authority. We still have laws here in the Soviet Union." The man took the rejection from my hands and said, "We'll have a look at it." I was back in the ring.

A Happy Death

My mother postponed her death by six months and was one of the few people who managed to die a happy death. She had a heart infarction and was admitted in the intensive care unit. I received a phone call in which I was told that her condition was critical. I wanted to leave immediately, but at that point I was living on the opposite side of the iron curtain, in Denmark, and back in the mid-1970s you couldn't just travel into the Soviet Union. A whole bunch of people would now have to make a number of fateful decisions as to whether, I, Shitty Couch, would be permitted to see my mother.

Most people think that Churchill was the one who coined the term "Iron Curtain" back in the 1940s. That's not true. The iron curtain was invented in medieval times. It was used in the theater world. Back then, the stage was illuminated with candles, and an iron curtain was lowered in case there was a fire, separating the stage from the audience. That same curtain was put in use by the Soviet Union. It was lowered in front of the socialist stage, separating the revolutionary act from a perplexed audience in the West. At times an impressed audience. The curtain remained lowered for seventy years.

Life behind the iron curtain was like living in a besieged fortress. You couldn't get in or out. Those besieged thought they were surrounded by enemies. All the countries that didn't belong to the "socialist camp" were enemies. It is very difficult to imagine nowadays that there are people on the planet who have no idea how other people live in other countries.

That was the kind of people we were back then. It was like in ancient times when people knew that way up north there lived people with dog heads. They had never been way up north. No one had been way up north. You could fabricate anything, since no one had the faintest idea what the truth was, only that poor workers were exploited by evil capitalists. That was the picture we had of the West. And we sympathized deeply with the Blacks in America because they were getting lynched.

There were very few cities which foreigners were allowed to visit. Our beautiful city, Leningrad, was one of those few. They smelled differently, wore different clothes. These people with dog heads.

The Iron Curtain wasn't made of solid iron. There were holes in it. Certain coveted objects, which people dreamed about, managed to penetrate through the gaps. Like pantyhose! The population dreamed about pantyhose! For some strange reason or other, they were not produced in the Soviet Union. The same with panties. We had underpants that reached half-way down your thigh until they ended with an elastic trim. When I was eighteen years old, I saw a package which was referred to as "the little week." It contained seven pairs of nylon panties in soft colors with a lace trim. They were French, a very coveted item. On the black market they cost the equivalent of two months of my mother's pension. Completely unattainable! But you could always dream. Soap from the West had a different scent. The scent of another life. And plastic bags! A colorful plastic bag from the West was a wonderful gift to receive. The colors of a different life.

Soviet citizens believed whole-heartedly that all who came from a capitalist country were capitalists. That was how we referred to them. Under the innocent name Beryozka, which means "little birch tree," a very special kind of shop was concealed, one to which "capitalists" alone had access. The only acceptable money was foreign currency from capitalist countries. The only thing about the shops that gave away the fact that they were special was their name. You couldn't see through the windows what was inside. There, the foreigners could buy liquor, cigarettes, furs, jewelry, caviar, and matryoshka nesting dolls, everything their hearts could desire.

The state alone controlled the monopoly to trade with foreign countries. If I, as a Russian, had a few American dollars in my possession and showed my money, I would have been taken aside, put under interrogation, perhaps been arrested and put in jail. In other more serious cases of possession of foreign exchange you could risk execution.

LP Records were very special commodities. That year, 1975, I had an order from friends in the USSR: Bad Company, Jeff Beck, Bachman Turner Overdrive, Queen, Nazareth, Deep Purple, Black Sabbath, Uriah Heep, The Sweet, Jethro Tull, Manfred Mann, Elton John, David Bowie, Emerson, Lake and Palmer, and Sparks. And bouillon cubes.

The system, after all, was not totally airtight. That's how you knew that pantyhose existed. But they were not available in the Soviet Union. There were heavy industries which manufactured locomotives, rockets, and tractors, but not consumer goods for the system's citizens.

It was also the year when my mother survived the blood clot in her heart. She came back from the hospital, called me, and said with difficulty, "Don't worry. I'll make sure not to die. I want to see my grandchild." I had my daughter, Anna, the previous year, and now we were waiting to get permission to come and visit my mother. We were rejected on the grounds that the trip was non-essential. It was the usual rejection, the language of the system whenever you tried to address the authorities.

There was a very specific procedure associated with crossing the border between socialism and capitalism. The procedure was known as "an invitation." If I, for example, wanted my mother to come visit me in Denmark, I would first have to write down on a piece of paper that I was inviting her and would pay for all costs in connection with her visit including medical treatment. Afterwards, the piece of paper had to be shown to the notary public, an individual who could confirm—if necessary—that you were who you claimed to be. The notary public would place a big red stamp that confirmed my signature. It made me feel like a very important individual—now I had a big red stamp, and one with a wax seal, at that. With the wax seal in my hands, I had to proceed to the Ministry of Foreign Affairs in order to obtain the next stamp in the process, an apostille, which was to confirm the stamp from the notary public. With the two very important stamps I was to proceed to the Russian Embassy, which looked at me and my stamps with contempt and confirmed the Danish Foreign Ministry's stamp with their own stamp.

The procedure was unnecessarily complicated because the Soviet state aimed to ostracize us. People like me, Shitty Couch, former citizen of the Soviet Union who had managed to cross to the other side of the iron curtain by their own unaided efforts and not because they had been officially sent there by the state, were by definition considered to be enemies of the people. The same procedure applied going the other way. If my mother wanted me to pay her a visit, it also entailed a very long procedure and in both instances you might get rejected.

I wrote a letter to OVIR, the department for visas and registration which was responsible for issuing permissions to travel abroad.

> *Honorable Head Comrade,*
> *I apologize for approaching you with a request*
> *but I have a feeling that only you can help me.*

> *My name is Sofia Vesterholt. My mother has delivered all the documents necessary to invite me and my husband, Ole Kristian Vesterholt, for a visit to Leningrad. It has been eight months and she has not received an answer. I have absolutely no desire to burden you with my letters, but unfortunately my mother is completely helpless. She is severely handicapped. She has had two brain clots and is paralyzed and has difficulty talking (she can't even call your office to hear if there is anything new). She only has me. She expects me to come. She has had a very hard life and has always worked hard. During the Siege of Leningrad, she continued to live and work in the city. Now she is disabled and has so little joy left in her life. I beg you to take a look at our case and, if it isn't too inconvenient for you, to send your response to Copenhagen and not to my mother because I fear that yet another rejection would be too much of a blow for her. She still hopes. I ask you with the greatest urgency to give me permission to visit my mother.*
>
> *With deference and hope I await your response and decision.*
>
> *Sofia Vesterholt*

Those of us who don't come from the West are accustomed to having to creep and crawl before the authorities, and hate them for it!

I was finally granted permission. I was given a tourist visa, which meant I was only allowed to take lodgings at a hotel. They made it very clear to me that I was not permitted to stay with my mother.

In my usual pangs of guilt over having left her, I consoled myself with the thought that by living in the West I was better able to help her. I had to attend to everything in her life, her rent, her food, and the assistance she received. Her pension was purely symbolic. You couldn't live off it. It was assumed that family members took care of one another. Imagine all the coveted items I could now bring from Denmark and sell in the Soviet Union.

I was always dragging a whole bunch of stuff with me that I could sell. This time I decided to bring knitting yarn, but you were only permitted to bring a few balls with you. I didn't know how to knit, but someone taught me how to rib stitch so I sat down and made a big and extremely ugly blanket. Then I took it to Russia and unraveled it when I got there.

You were not permitted to bring books from the West, especially the ones in Russian which people were forbidden to read in the Soviet Union. It could, for example, be Solzhenitsyn, Russian authors who emigrated to the West during the revolution—or the Bible or any other religious literature in Russian.

You weren't allowed to bring letters *out* of the Soviet Union, nor old photographs. If someone got the idea to write a letter and send it abroad, they would have to send it by post so that it could be properly monitored. I was often asked to bring letters out to the West. I always had to think up new hiding places until finally I came up with something brilliant. No, I'm not the one who invented the fax machine or emails. This was way before anything like that existed. What I did do several times was paste letters under my foot using a wide, skin-colored band-aid. One time I was pulled aside by the Customs, searched, and asked to remove all my clothes. There I was, standing on a letter written by a friend to her old aunt in New York, feeling triumphant because they didn't manage to find it.

> A man is being interrogated by the KGB. The officer says, "You have a brother who lives abroad." Yes, the man confirms, guilt-ridden. "He has written to you many times." Yes, the man confirms once again. "Why haven't you answered him? How do you explain that?" The man shrugs his shoulders. The officer pushes a piece of paper and a pen toward him. "Here you are. Write to your brother now." The man takes the pen and starts writing. "My dear brother, I have finally managed to find the time and place to write this letter..."

That summer we were all in the countryside. The weather was gorgeous, and we had a wonderful and cozy time. Family, friends, and acquaintances sat laughing in the kitchen. A KGB vehicle was constantly parked out on the road, and we all pretended not to notice it. There was so much joy that summer. The tiniest thing could bring immense joy. My mother was constantly laughing. You can easily be paralyzed and at the same time happy. I remember my mother's crooked mouth that distorted when she laughed. Little did we know that those days would be the final ones of her life.

That summer my mother finally met her granddaughter who had turned one year old while we had been waiting for permission to enter the USSR. They smiled a lot to each other. They both had a dimple in their right cheek.

We were together for ten days, and then my mother fell ill and had to go to the hospital. The last night it was raining. I sat by her bed reading a newspaper. She woke up and said, "Imagine, I dreamt I was in a kindergarten. Suddenly it was flooding and the small pieces of children's furniture started floating around. It was so funny." I said, "That's because it's raining outside." My mother replied, "The summer rain lightens everything." She was sixty-one years old, she had been paralyzed in the last fifteen years of her life, had survived the revolution, terror, war, famine, siege, and the persecution of the Jews, and now she had a very high temperature.

I asked, "Do you want me to wash you?" as I filled a bucket of water. "Remember to put in the perfume," she said. I had brought her French perfume from Denmark. I added it and washed her. "How do you feel now?" I asked her. She looked at me and said with a smile and a sigh of relief, "Oh, I feel so very wonderful." She looked aside, and in that very second she passed away. My mother died with relief and a smile on her lips.

Burying a person in the Soviet Union wasn't easy either. You had to get ahold of a coffin. Just like everything else, you couldn't just buy it, you had to procure it. I needed permission to bury my mother in a Jewish cemetery in the same plot as my maternal grandfather whom I had never met. He had been the Chief Rabbi in the old Russian town of Pskov. After the revolution the family had moved to Leningrad where they had erased all traces of their past. In 1929 a law had been promulgated denying all descendants of nobility and ecclesiastical figures the right of higher education. So that was why my family kept a secret. My grandpa had been a Rabbi, something I didn't know until I was twenty.

All families had their secrets. Throughout your life, you constantly had to fill out questionnaires for personnel departments. There were a number of questions that could "invalidate" you for the rest of your life. You could at any given point have a wrong nationality, all depending on whom the government happened to be persecuting and when. At times, entire nationalities were deported. Train carriages full of guilty nationalities were transported through the territories of the Soviet Union to distant regions. If you had relatives abroad, it was considered a great crime. If you had resided on German occupied territory during the War, it was also a crime. One

of the questions was whether you had ever been arrested—
imagine that in a country that has experienced wave after wave
of terror. The constant fear of being revealed was always lurking. All families had something to hide. But what was worse?

To have an aunt in France, or to be of Jewish
descent?

To have been on German-occupied territory, or
to be a descendant of a nobleman?

To be a Tatar, or to have spent fifteen days in jail
because of public drunkenness?

People who have bad breath can't smell how bad it is.
In the same way, we couldn't always sense the eternal fear we
harbored. It was buried so deeply within us that there was still
space for experiencing joy in one's work, partying, and love.
You could be guilty in so many ways. Our family was lucky. It
was just that we were Jews.

It took a long time to get permission to bury my mother.
The summer was very hot, and the little mortuary in the hospital where she lay ran out of ice. In order to ensure that her
body didn't begin to disintegrate before the funeral, I went
into town, to Leningrad, and found a medical student. He
agreed to remove the most perishable parts of her body in
return for some LPs from the West. Bad Company and Deep
Purple really came in handy. We were given permission by
a kind hospital administrator to perform it quickly and discreetly, which meant that we had to come in during the night.

There were two little rooms in the small mortuary. In one
of them, my mother lay naked on a table. In the other, I sat
keeping an eye and making sure no one came while the medical student performed the procedure. Afterwards, we had to
clean everything up, and then I could dress my mother and
apply make-up on her. I applied the French perfume all over
her body once again and dressed her in a silk outfit which I had
brought from Denmark and which she had worn every day of

the last ten days before she was hospitalized. And pantyhose. My mother had to have those damned pantyhose on—as a last greeting from the free world. The medical student helped me dress her. I had promised her many times that, when she died, I would apply make-up on her and make sure she was well dressed. In Russia you part with the deceased while they are lying in an open coffin.

We quietly left the room with a bucket that had to be emptied at a specifically assigned spot. Under my arm I was carrying four brightly colored LPs from the West. On the black market, they were worth more than an average monthly salary each.

My Father

Dear Sonya,
Your father is very sick. Could you perhaps go to the embassy and ask what would be needed for you to get a visa to come here? They could easily verify how ill he is and the fact that he received a medal for fifty years of loyal membership in the Communist Party, which must mean something. The District Party Committee came to honor him with it. What if a telegram were sent from the hospital? Would that help? He wants so badly to see you. You know how much it means to him to receive a visit from you. The people employed at the embassy are also human, after all, and must be able to sympathize with a cancer patient.
Send my love to everyone,
Lara

Lara, my father's wife, and I had each from our vantage point implored the Soviet authorities in hopes that I would receive an entry permit and see him one last time. At that point I had been living in Denmark for thirteen years and had obtained Danish citizenship. At first, when I got to Denmark, the KGB was hopeful that they could establish a fruitful collaboration with me. Finally, it dawned on them that I had absolutely no intention of cooperating with them, and then the hammer fell. I didn't behave nicely. That was something I had to be punished for. From that point on, my visa applications were rejected, as they continued to be until the collapse of the Soviet Union. There was no mercy.

Lara assumed that her letters to me would be censored. That was the usual way in the Soviet Union if you sent a letter to or received one from abroad. Other eyes were also reading along. The people's contact with foreign countries was to be monitored. So, she wasn't only writing her letters to me, but also to those who issued visas, those who read the letters who had control and power, in an attempt to appeal to them so that they would take pity on us. Look, she wrote, he has been a loyal member of the Party for fifty years. Doesn't he deserve to receive a visit from his daughter? Those of you who are reading this letter, you are also human and must have some understanding of the situation.

Lara was my father's last wife, his third, I thought, but in reality, she was his fourth—something I first discovered when I started writing this book. The only thing I knew was that before my mother there had been another woman, Luba, with whom he had had two children. Then he met my mother and moved in with her, had me, moved back in with Luba, whom he then married and later divorced, then he moved back in with my mother, whom he left when she became paralyzed, and then he married a third woman, namely, Lara. I had no idea that long before those three women there had been another woman in his life, and that she and their only child had died in childbirth.

He left my mother the first time when I was around five years old and returned when I was nine. He was the kind of man who had to have food on the table as soon as he walked in the door from work, and he would scream and shout at my mother if it wasn't ready. Three courses. Food shortages in the Soviet Union in no way reflected on the variety of dishes conjured up as a result of the fantasy and selflessness of Russian housewives.

My mother would rush back and forth during supper. As soon as the table was set in our room, she would spurt out to the hallway, turn right, turn right again into the kitchen, reemerge moments later carrying a potful of steaming sour cabbage soup, and rush into our room. Sour cabbage soup, stew, and stewed fruit. Those were the most common dishes. The food had to be hot, of course, and, were she to get distracted between the soup and the main dish by a neighbor out in the kitchen, my father would sit fuming with rage at the table and would shout in her face when she finally reappeared. It was like the zoo, when the lion had to be fed. The blissful aromas from the kitchen would float toward the animal's quivering nostrils. Eight housewives, each at their burner, cooking three-course-meals for their eight animals who all sat growling and expectant at the tables in their cages.

Usually, soup is included in the menu, which covers the requirement for liquids. You don't usually drink anything with your meal in Russia, and I'm not referring to vodka. Drinking water with your food is unheard of, not the least because tap water isn't pure. And the idea of actually boiling water and cooling it off to drink it with your meal is considered downright absurd. Tea? Sandwiches go with that.

Diametrically opposed to Russian custom, my father wanted a specific kind of mineral water with his meal. A Borjomi from Georgia, with snow-covered mountains on the label. It was, of course, very hard to obtain.

It wasn't far from the table to the piano, it was just a matter of turning around really. So, when he was done digesting his food, my father would sit down and perform Schumann's *Ich grolle nicht*, to his own accompaniment.

> *I bear no grudge, though my heart is breaking,*
> *O love forever lost! I bear no grudge.*
> *(Translation by Richard Stokes)*

Music was a big part of our lives. We had a piano in our twelve square meters, and my parents played it and sang together a lot. Classical music. Duets. "Why are you putting on such airs?" I used to think as I cringed with embarrassment. I saw a cultural gap between them, with their duets by Rossini, and the rest of the neighbors in our *kommunalka* apartment where a bunch of housewives were cooking borscht in the kitchen. Especially when they got to the cat duet, I'd quickly sneak off into the hallway or the bathroom. "Meow-meow" could be heard seeping through all the cracks. I mostly felt like hiding myself deep within those cracks so I didn't have to hear all of those cat cries.

Apart from that, my father was a totally ordinary joyful household tyrant. He was always the natural center of attraction at any gathering. He was a Party member since 1931, but he never talked about politics within the walls of his own home. Not a single word. He had nothing to say regarding parades, speeches, or political decisions. Neither did he ever talk about how he managed to survive the Great Terror or what it was like to be a Jew in an antisemitic country. For a man who was thoroughly talkative through and through, exuberant, and witty, he was uncommonly silent when it came to "-isms," whether it was communism, antisemitism, or Stalinism.

But did I expect of him? That he, as a dedicated member of the Communist Party, had something he needed to get off his chest, something he wanted to discuss, clarify, tell his daughter? I never asked him, and the silence was mutual. He and his generation, the ones who had been children during the revolution, continued their lives after Stalin's death as though nothing had occurred. I belonged to the new and exuberant Soviet generation that perceived the communist ideology as one big deception, a generation that communicated through jokes, dealing with the absurdity of the system and all its shortcomings.

My beloved fatherland could sometimes resemble a blind man in a locked room who is desperately trying to find a way out. He runs into the walls, bruises himself bloody, and tries running in a different direction only to ram into a wardrobe and bruise himself even bloodier. He is looking for a way out, for a better life, but time and again runs his head against a brick wall. Each time he starts all over again. If I were to compare my father's upbringing with my own, there is a real risk that history would repeat itself.

The era of the tsars was the firing shot for the Russian Revolution. There was a desire to move away from oppression and inequality. My father was ten years old when the revolution broke out in 1917 and fifteen when the Soviet Union was established. In a class picture dating from 1925 he and his classmates are bursting with expectations for the future. You can see it in their faces. My father's generation was born to experience the revolution and move from oppression toward hope. For their part, their enthusiastic hopes and dreams of happiness resulted in forty years of lies, terror, and genocide. The path to a communist paradise was a dead-end street.

Then came the next generation. I was born while Stalin was still alive and eight years old when he died. As teenagers, my peers and I were told that all the atrocities that had occurred under Stalin had been a mistake. Our generation was given a new sense of hope. A date was even set for the coming of paradise. In the year of our Lord 1980 communism was to become a reality. But nothing happened, thank goodness, only that people were now allowed to have a cow and that we sent someone out into space. Other than that, the oppression of the people continued as though nothing had happened. The first path to happiness had ended in a blood bath, the second one ended in resignation.

In the 1930s, my father was already well established: he was married, had two children, a good job as head of a department in the Naval Forces Research Institute in Leningrad, and was a member of the Party. But his then wife, Luba, must have heard the drums of the Great Terror approaching and sensed the ground shaking underneath them. She tried to make him quit his job. As long as he was invisible and wasn't sitting in a high position, the chances of surviving were better.

> *When the bloodthirsty cha glares at you from the thickets, become a shadow, and the nose of the cha will not smell your blood. When the ikhi swoops down from the pink clouds, become a shadow, and the eyes of the ikhi will search for you in the grass in vain. When, in the light of the two moons—olio and litkha—the evil spider tsitli spins its web around your dwelling, become a shadow, and the tsitli will not catch you. Become a shadow, poor son of Tuma.*
> (Excerpt from the novel Aelita. The plot takes place on Mars ... Translation by Lucy Flaxman)

My father survived. He did as Luba said, thereby possibly avoiding the fate that, by contrast, befell many others—from all strata of society and often completely randomly—namely, that of being shot or sent to the Gulag because "they had committed an act that was dangerous for society."

During the War, he was in the army and would transport supplies to Leningrad as the Germans surrounded the city. The only way you could reach Leningrad with supplies and leave again with people was by crossing the frozen Ladoga Lake, a dangerous route, which was referred to as "The Road of Life." Bombs fell, the ice would break, and cars would fall through the ice and sink. Carrying vital supplies. Carrying people who hoped that they could escape from the hellish cold and the famine. Those that who managed to escape would sometimes end up eating far too much far too quickly and die anyway.

The Second World War was, oddly, a time of relief for some, a break from the ideological madness of Communism. Death had literally been knocking on the door for years. At night. Ever since the revolution, Lenin, Stalin, the Great Terror. The state conducted its arrests in the dark, and the fear of falling asleep at night was ingrained in millions of citizens.

There are many ways you can fear death. An invisible creature may be on board your spaceship and you have no idea where or when it will attack you. But now there was suddenly a very solid and above all visible enemy: namely, Fascist Germany. Phew, so it was no longer only the Soviet Union that was eating itself from within and randomly murdering "the enemy of the people." In this respite from the fear, many Russians were prepared to sacrifice their own lives, not so that communism would triumph but in order to save their country and their families. My father was one of them.

My parents met in Leningrad during the Siege. I have this idea that he may have saved her from starving to death and that he may have shared his rations with her, but I'm not entirely sure. All I know is that they stuck together during the entire period of the War, had a love child together, me, and triumphed together in the Great War of the Fatherland. Carried by the march of triumph, we arrived in Germany where our little family had a happy time. We were the conquerors and were given a big room to live in.

New Year's, 1946. I have a picture from that time with my father, mother, my mother's two friends whom she met in Germany, and a whole bunch of other people. Everyone is standing in accordance with the directions of the photographer and wearing funny hats. Why, though? That's not a Russian tradition at all, and certainly not something you would do in the USSR. Perhaps it had been my German nanny, Bertha, who had introduced them because I immediately recognized the funny hats the first time I celebrated

New Year's in Denmark. In the picture there are festoons and streamers everywhere. Golden rain, as tinsel is called in Russian, hangs in abundance from a big Christmas tree that reaches all the way to the ceiling. My parents are in foreign surroundings, and it is as though the light of New Year's Eve shines on them, a harbinger of good things for the coming year.

Where am I in the picture? I had probably been put to bed already, but the wondering intonation of the question is leading my brain a little astray because within it there is a whole universe of jokes simply waiting for a cue, a code, like a bank box. Each joke has its own bank box. "Where am I in the picture?"—click—and the door to one of the bank boxes opens.

> The Polish Communists are going to celebrate their anniversary, and the Soviet Union would like to present a gift. But what? They decide to commission a painting by a very famous painter. It is to be called, "Lenin Is in Poland." The members of the Central Committee go to Poland with the gift. At the reception, the picture is covered with a white cloth. The foreman for the Central Committee of the Soviet Union makes a speech and unveils the gift. He pulls off the cloth, and a huge *gasp* is heard throughout the hall. There is utter silence. The picture portrays Lenin's wife in bed with the KGB's commander-in-chief. No one knows where to look, but finally someone dares to say what everyone is thinking. "Where is Lenin in the picture?" he asks, to which he is given the answer, "Lenin? Lenin is in Poland!"

My father brought the two children from his previous marriage to Germany. They had survived the horrors of the War in miserable conditions in the eastern regions of the Soviet

Union, where they had been evacuated together with their mother, Luba. Now the children moved in with us and would attend school. There was nothing strange about that. Wartime is not like ordinary times. It was not uncommon for men and women to start new relationships even though they already had families. My mother received the children with open arms, and I myself shouted for joy when I ran to meet them as they climbed the steps to our home.

In 1950 we returned to Leningrad—my mother and I to a small room, my father to Luba together with my half-siblings. But the country was sick and had been so for a long time. Antisemitism is like a herpes outbreak. There's no vaccine against it. In Stalin's final years, the illness flared up and persecution of the Jews broke out into bright flames. My father had to flee with Luba and the children.

> *When the bloodthirsty cha glares at you from the thickets, become a shadow, and the nose of the cha will not smell your blood. When the ikhi swoops down from the pink clouds, become a shadow, and the eyes of the ikhi will search for you in the grass in vain.*

They traveled to the Far East, to Kholmsk on the Sakhalin Peninsula. You couldn't have gotten further away from Leningrad. Eleven thousand kilometers eastward. Across twelve longitudinal degrees. A quarter of the entire globe. When Stalin died and the persecution of the Jews faded away, my father returned to Leningrad—and to my mother.

The apex of his life was the production of the world's first atomically driven icebreaker, *Lenin*. He was a part of the managing committee. When the ship was launched, I was there to witness my father's great triumph. The families of the men in the managing committee were given the honor of getting a tour of the colossal icebreaker. With great enthusiasm, my mother and I followed the procession that wormed itself around the inside of *Lenin*. I never got to see any reactors, but there was a white grand piano on board and a frying pan that could fry two hundred meatballs.

That evening there was a party. My father was once again the center of attention, bubbly as always when everyone's eyes were on him. He also told a joke that evening, a completely innocent one.

It is spring. The ground is fresh, black, and soft from the rain. Everything is fragrant. A small earthworm emerges from the ground. It looks around as the warm rays of the sun pour down on it. Suddenly it catches sight of another earthworm and says, "You're very cute. So pink, so adorable! Maybe you and I should get together?"

At which point my mother couldn't help interrupting him: "Oh, you idiot," she continued jubilantly, "don't you realize I'm your other end?"

She should never have said that. In the very distinguished gathering in honor of the icebreaker my poor mother had given away the punch line. My father was furious. That night, as we took the trolley home, he didn't look at her once. Just sat peering out the window into the darkness as we rattled along. Under his arm he was carrying the gift which had been presented to him. A framed photo of the model of the icebreaker *Lenin*. He didn't speak to my mother in the following days. She had upset his apple cart. Broken the string of spontaneous attention which was always allotted to him in a gathering.

At home my father removed the picture from the frame, and in my childish handwriting I listed *Lenin*'s impressive facts on the back of it. Length: 134 meters, breadth: 27,6 meters, displacement: 16000 tons, descent: 10.5 meters, four turbines each containing 11,000 horsepower; can penetrate a

2.5-meter-thick icesheet, whereas an ordinary icebreaker can only penetrate a 0.5-meter-thick icesheet; can pull a convoy of ships through the Arctic. Whereupon he placed the photo back in the frame and put in the display cabinet in our twelve-square-meter home.

The state had a tendency to reward its subjects with certain privileges. It could be packages with food, living quarters, or permission to do some thing or other that was normally forbidden. It would reward them with something that was fundamentally human. And if it took back those rewards, the subjects were easily manageable. We all have the need to be able to call something "ours." When you have to obtain living quarters, normally you do so according to your abilities and the money you have, but in a totalitarian state, which distributed everything, you were constantly pestered with the idea that the distribution must be administered fairly amongst the people. That's why calculations were constantly being made. It was the same sort of thinking as when I as a child lay in my foldout bed dreaming about winning a car. What could I do with all the money that I'd get if I sold it? The numbers accumulated in one calculation after the other, pushing Tolstoy and science fiction out of the bed.

We were eligible for new living quarters. One could remain in that state for thirty or forty years. However, some work places were sometimes allotted a certain number of apartments. Because my father had contributed to something honorable through his efforts in the production of the icebreaker *Lenin*, he was given the one great reward of his life: a two-room apartment. And after he got that, he left us.

Perhaps he felt that he could justify leaving us. My mother had had a stroke and had become paralyzed, he had started a relationship with a female colleague at his workplace, and now he had bought his indulgence by way of the apartment. We had an impressive twenty-seven square meters in the world's largest country. Nine square meters for each of us, according to the new rules. A total of twenty-seven square meters on one-sixth of the globe.

> The Soviet territory consisted of 22,000,000 square kilometers, which, converted to square meters, equals 22, 000,000,000,000. There lived 220,000,000 people in the Soviet Union. Had there been any form of justice, the calculation would have looked like this: 22,000,000,000,000 : 220,000,000 = 100,000 square meters for every Soviet citizen, including steppes, deserts, taigas, and rivers.

I would at any given moment give up 30,000 square meters of steppes, 50,000 square meters of rivers, and an entire desert for just one additional square meter of living space in Leningrad.

Any other man would have seized the opportunity to exchange the apartment for a room for himself and his new wife and a room for his daughter and ex-wife. But not my father. He declined the possibility to do that. In Soviet families where you clung to each and every square meter that you could possibly get ahold of, he went from one woman to another to a third without taking his rightful number of square meters with him. Not doing so was considered by many to be a heroic deed—equal to saving a child or fighting for the fatherland.

My mother could have complained about his leaving her to the Party organization at his workplace. She even received a phone call from a "well-intentioned" individual from my father's workplace who tried to persuade her to send in a complaint about him to the Party organization. That was back when the Party could meddle in just about anything. She passed up the opportunity. She was damn well a hero, as well!

> A woman sends a letter to her husband's work place in which she writes that she is broken-hearted because her husband neglects his marital responsibilities. The husband is summoned to appear before the Party Committee. The chairman says to him, "Comrade, we have received a complaint from your wife. She claims that you neglect her and don't fulfil your matrimonial duties." The husband defends himself, "Yes, but it's not my fault. I can't. I'm impotent." The chairman stands up, slams his fist hard down on the table, and says, "Comrade! You are first and foremost a member of the Communist Party! You must!"

After my parents' divorce I always sensed the extended hand of my father reaching toward me. We received a little money from him each month, even though he could only give us very, very little. But everyone had very little back then. When we would meet, he was always drowning in guilt and trying to justify his actions by explaining why he had abandoned his sick wife. "Back when we returned from Germany, " he once said, "I had a big stamp collection and she just gave it away. She would give everything away." All his colorful stamps with animals and birds, buildings, and people from countries all over the world. I sometimes wonder whether she had given his dreams to someone else. When I visited him and his new wife, he behaved as before, singing songs and telling jokes. But he was aware that I knew him to be guilty of abandoning my sick mother.

Getting sick in Russia has always been a family affair. Both then and now. It's not just a moral duty. The family simply has no other choice. There is no one else who can help.

When my father abandoned us, I was the only one left with my mother. But then I abandoned her as well, got married, and left for Denmark. I paid for her care, and in that my father and I were even. Now we were both criminals, guilty of having abandoned the same woman.

> *My dear Sonya,*
> *It was wonderful reading your letter. I must admit that I've read it several times (which isn't typical of me). I sense that you are happy. I have so many thoughts in mind but for some reason or other I can't seem to get them down on paper. The problem is that one wants to write some affectionate words, something I'm not very good at. So many times in my life I've heard false words and untruthful outpourings, and so, when the affectionate words make themselves felt and "want to come out of me," it doesn't matter how genuine they may be, I become defiant in the face of them and growl like an angry dog, even though I know perfectly well that hearing affectionate words does everyone good. But all of this is "pathetic nonsense" and the delirious talk of an old man.*
>
> *I'm trying to imagine your new life and am envisioning how your eyes and ears must be absorbing everything. You want to hear and see everything. I myself have once trekked through foreign cities with the same eagerness, actually, through many cities. Imagine, from north to south (Murmansk, Arkhangelsk, Odessa, Kiev, Baku, Tbilisi, Sevastopol), from west to east (Riga, Tallinn, Vilnius, Vladivostok, Khabarovsk, Sakhalin, Kamchatka), and everything in between. I've also been thinking about*

the three years that we lived in Germany. It was a very exciting time, and things were good for us, from the material point of view. Yet still I learned to understand, which I hadn't before then, what it means to suffer from homesickness. East or West, home is best. Not only in the way of life and habits, but also in personalities and language, in nature and in the human condition, things aren't the way one was used to from one's childhood. Different are all the things that are an integral part of one's psyche.

My little daughter, write to me and tell me whether you will visit our embassy. I think it would be a nice thing for you to do. They most likely have a library and recent newspapers and journals and I hope that you will have the chance to celebrate the October Revolution together with some of your own countrymen.

We are doing well. Your mother is on medication. I myself am doing well and am looking forward to your letters. I am happy that you are critical of everything you experience, even though it is all new and you are so happy to be together with your beloved. You are critical of their films and you are right to be. Our films are, of course, for the most part, better.

I often think of Ole. He is so good-natured, and I am happy that you are together with him and that you two get on so well. You must send him many greetings from me. In general, you know how highly I regard the Danes. I think the people in this little country are people with a capital "P." Their lives are based on humanism, mutual respect, good upbringing, and tact. I am certain that you have the same qualities and will easily be able to gain the respect of your new family.

Thank you so much for remembering my hobby and pasting those impressive looking stamps with ships on the envelope. I'll do the same thing because I am certain that there are members of your new family or children of some of your neighbors who would take delight in them. Write to me. Perhaps some of them collect stamps on certain themes: flora, fauna, art, ships, Lenin, portraits, technology, etc. Then I'll select the stamps based on those themes.

Take care, my little girl. I'm sending you a kiss. Say hello to your father-in-law, your husband, and his family whom I, even though I don't know them, deeply respect.
Your father

This was the first letter I received from him after I had traveled to a capitalist country. As a result, there emerged an entirely new form of communication between us. Now I was sitting in Denmark and knew that he knew that I knew that he wasn't only writing for my benefit but also for other eyes. To them he was saying: My daughter is innocent. She has left in order to be together with her beloved, not because she prefers capitalism to communism, and, make no mistake, she is viewing her new life with a critical gaze.

My father was a member of the Party. His letter is a tour de force in the art of justification to the Soviet government. Were other governments any better than the Soviet? Was the Danish state? Didn't they also open letters from abroad and read them before they delivered them to the recipients? He couldn't be certain, so, to be on the safe side, he tried to ingratiate himself with the Danes: you are kind, you are good, you are nice. Treat her well, she will most certainly behave.

In the first phase after I had left the Soviet Union there was still the possibility of visiting my family and friends, until the KGB lost their patience with me and our family and our communications were reduced to letters and telephone calls. The government was involved in everything that we did, so it was entirely up to them whether I would be given permission to visit my parents. Just imagine, the government alone decided whether I could see my father and mother, embrace them, go for walks with them, eat together with them, do completely ordinary everyday things with them. The punishment that the KGB imposed on those individuals who refused to collaborate with the government sent large ripples out into the water, resulting in numerous human tragedies. I was denied an entry permit and couldn't come when my family was screaming for help.

> *My dear Sonya,*
> *I was so happy to receive your letter. Please send Ole my heartfelt congratulations on finishing his studies of several years. How impressive that he now holds a master's degree. And I can't hide the fact that being able to tell my friends that my daughter teaches at Copenhagen University makes me proud. Of course it isn't good to boast, but nothing human is foreign to me. Now all I want to do is to command, as we do in the Navy, "Full speed ahead," and wish you both "Bon voyage."*
>
> *I am sending both of you kisses. I always wait for news, letters, and to hear of your arrival.*
> *Your father*

My dear girl,
Thank you for the map of Copenhagen with all your detailed descriptions and thank you so much for the presents. They made a huge impression. The entire family, the neighbors, and our friends applaud your taste. I received many telegrams on my seventieth birthday, and an old colleague came by. On behalf of the management, he handed over a three-liter electric samovar with an engraving.

Sonyechka, you write so seldom, and I am worried. Just write a few lines to me. I'm growing old, it is inevitable and unavoidable.

Like I said, I am sending you and little Anna kisses and embrace Ole.
Your father

My dear girl,
Every day, morning and night, I go down to the mailbox, full of hope, only to return in disappointment. Every night until the early hours I write letters to you in my mind but I can't get my thoughts and feelings down on paper. Sleeping pills don't help me to fall asleep. I am so sad, my girl. Forgive me for changing from my usual noncomplaining self. That is most likely why it has always looked as though my life is in order. And perhaps I seemed "guilty" because I never sought any sympathy and have never accused anyone of the problems I myself had enough of. I often think of Schumann's ballad Ich grolle nicht: "Even though you have forgotten me, I am not angry."

I understand you, my child, you are working hard, not in order to save money but to spend it generously and because you can't settle for a rou-

tine-based lifestyle but want to throw yourself in all sorts of new directions. You'll never be of the bourgeoisie, neither mentally nor materially. How I wish I could be together with you just for a few days so I could tell you about myself, perhaps justify my actions, but fate has decreed it otherwise. It would make me happy if you could come, but I don't dare hope for it.
Your father

My beloved Sonya,
I sense that I am slowly but surely reaching the finish line. I want so badly to "find" you, and the feeling grows stronger and stronger for each day. I formulate it in my letters but feel that that isn't how I should write it down. You don't like melodrama. Forgive me, I can't do this in any other way. I have no funny words or funny thoughts to share. I want to complain, but I have no one to complain to. I blame myself, recall all my many faults and stupidities, my incredible simple-mindedness, my fits of hysteria. And what good does it do? I can't redo it. Forgive me, my beloved child. I beg you, drop me a line. I am old and sick, but still alive.
Your father

My dear Sonyechka,
On March 10 I had a stroke and have been to the hospital but am feeling better now. I thought I would kick the bucket. Lara has to take two months off from work in order to care of me and I will have to swallow all of my pride and ask you for your help if it doesn't inconvenience you too

*much. Would you please call me when you receive the letter? I can't pay for the phone call because when I called you on your birthday it cost thirty rubles. And your present (once again, thank you so much) I will need to use to cover the bill for my teeth. If you get a chance to visit us, I want to remind you that you need to start with our embassy in Denmark.
Your father*

*Sonyechka,
I have now spoken to you on the telephone and felt immediately better. My dear daughter, damn it (imagine a broad array of sailors' phrases), you are removing yourself more and more from me, and it is getting harder and harder for me to bear, but I will not get offended. I could never be angry with you, most probably because you are the most important person in my life. (I am sorry for being so pathetic, but I can't help it). I want to know everything you wish to tell me. What kind of an apartment do you live in? What kind of people do you meet with? What places do you visit? How is work coming along? What do the prospects for it look like, your plans and expectations?*

My dear one, for God's sake, don't leave me. You must understand that it is much too expensive for me to call you. Every call corresponds to 1½–2 days' worth of my pension. That is why I am asking you: write to me.

*Hugs and kisses—I am always waiting for you to come.
Your father*

My dear daughter,

I am writing from the hospital where I find myself once again. My health is playing tricks on me. I am neither coming or going, but you would say that I'm putting on airs. Okay, go ahead and laugh at me, then, but I prefer everything being funny as opposed to sad. Even though it isn't funny.

I am now continuing the letter after a two-month hiatus. On October 13 I returned home from the hospital, and I have just celebrated my seventy-second birthday, Yesterday I was out for the first time since I've been sick. Now, I can walk, and see, and hear and don't need to be helped by others. I don't complain and maintain a cheerful spirit. I've now managed three times to cheat the Grim Reaper. That is to say, as a Ukrainian song goes, "As long as there is a spark in my eyes, let me live, let me live."

When I think back on the past, I blame myself for my numerous blunders—whether through words or actions—which were most likely a result of my emotions and irritability and the fact that I don't understand the thoughts or emotions of others, even though I may have had the best of intentions in the given situation. I must admit that you are the only person to whom I feel the need to justify my actions, which is an impossible thing to do through letter-writing.

If we ever meet each other again I will most likely cry on your shoulder and perhaps feel better again. If I don't live long enough to see the day then it's all the same. I don't remember whether I told you that both your aunts, my sisters, Zhenya and Galya, have passed away.

Forgive me for sending you this sad letter. I've read it through and am very dissatisfied with myself.

Wishing a Happy New Year's to you, and little Anna and Ole. I wish you health and happiness. Your father, still awaiting photos and letters with great anticipation!

Sonyechka,
I have found you on the map, my little girl. I take bus number 2, 3, or 29 to Thorvaldsens Street, turn right at your little street, K. M. Theiles Street, enter number 4 and climb to the first floor, ring the bell on the door to the left, and see your broad smile and astonished eyes.

Next door is Thorvaldsens School. There is a fifteen-minute walk to Nørrebro Street and approximately the same distance to Vesterbo Street. And an approximate twenty-five-minute walk to the zoo. Wonderful.

The news that you two have separated makes me sad but doesn't surprise me. I am very fond of Ole. You can't help but respect his Nordic calmness and ability to remain focused. He is a bit of a loner. He is also a goal-oriented man and exceptionally tactful, which are, of course, very commendable features. But these features have proven difficult to reconcile with your need to socialize and your thirst for everything new. You know what is best for you. My only wish is for you to be happy. Deep down I hope that both of you end up missing each other and that it happens before your period of separation terminates.
Your father

My dear little Sonya,

This year has proven particularly unfortunate for us. First, I had a stroke but I managed to recover from it without any impairment. Then, I was hospitalized in order to get some treatment for my bad legs. (Lara managed to get ahold of the medication.) As soon as I was discharged, Lara was hospitalized for the removal of a tumor in her breast, but luckily it went well because it turned out to be benign. Afterwards, I became sick once again. I had constant hiccups with heartburn and vomiting. A medical examination revealed that it was an organic constriction of the lowest third of the esophagus. It would require a major operation, which, combined with all my other ailments, I wouldn't be able to survive. On August 23 I am going to be hospitalized at the Radiological Institute for radiation therapy. They say it should help.

Sweet Sonya, please be so kind as to write to me when you are coming, or call.

I am sending you kisses,
You father

Little Sonya,

Come as soon as you can. I was given very little hope when we were at the hospital. Everything depends on how he responds to the radiation treatment.

Much love,
Lara

My dear Sonya,
Let me try to explain the situation the way things look now. Your father has been treated at the

Institute for X-Ray and Radiology. He underwent two radiation treatments using cobalt therapy from August 29 to September 30, then he was sent home for ten days, and went back again to the hospital from October 10 to November 1. He is home now. In the beginning of January he is scheduled for a follow-up at the hospital. Over and above the harsh nature of the treatment and the pain, he has been plagued by constant hiccups that don't stop even at night. There is nothing that we can do about it, and he suffers greatly. He has also lost quite a bit of weight because his appetite has disappeared after the treatment. And he is scared that, if he eats anything, the pain will only get worse. Even though his discharge papers may state that he has esophageal ulcers, he is an educated person and knows perfectly well that he has cancer as he has been assigned to an oncologist. He was in a deep depression and tried to cut both his wrists. Sonyechka, it is so horrible. He is suffering so terribly. I feel so sorry for him. I called in a good psychiatrist who treated him both for his depression and his hiccups. He feels a little better now and hasn't had hiccups for six days already. He has also started eating a little more. A nurse comes, who is, by good fortune, our neighbor, comes and gives him injections every evening. In general, Sonyechka, I am fighting with all my might and no one knows what's going to happen. He is very weak and doesn't want to do anything. He is completely apathetic. What are your plans? How are you? He wants so badly to see you and keeps saying that he probably won't live long enough to see you again. Please write and tell us your plans. On December 10 he will turn seventy-five, if...

I wish you all the best. Say hi to Ole and kiss little Anna. We await your letter with great anticipation.
Lara

My dear daughter,
I am very sick, so Lara is going to write instead of me.

My dear Sonyechka,
Every day we want to write to you, but your father's hands refuse to obey him. I am so busy and time just flies by. First and foremost, there is the state of your father's health. We are now in the second year after his first radiation treatment. We have been to the follow-up and there are some minor issues with the blood supply to his heart, but we hope that everything will straighten itself out. Everything would be bearable now, but every so often he gets hiccups that continue for three to five days at a time, even if he gets the tranquilizer injections. He lies down a little, and I scold him and force him to bring the matches from the room to the kitchen just to get him to move a little. His appetite is normal, but the other day his upper bridge fell out so he will have to get dentures.

The weather is constantly terrible. Either it's slippery outside, or it's raining, or there are heavy winds. We will have to wait for a couple of weeks to get the dentures so that he may have teeth by summertime.

Little Sonya, thank you so much for everything. I often wear the sweater you sent me, and Irina was so touched that you had sent her a pair of pants. They fit her perfectly. Time passes. The children are growing and you have also grown older.

Life has passed so quickly! I was recently looking at some old photographs and found a picture where we were all at the beach together. My dear girl, how quickly time flies, and your father neither sings nor dances anymore. Thank you for your pictures. You are in your prime, treat every day as a gift.

We await your letters with great anticipation. Today is the fortieth anniversary of the end of the Siege of Leningrad. I just hope there won't be a war.
Lara

Dear Lara,
Forgive me, but I have no more energy left. The illness is exhausting me. The doctor was right when he said it won't get better. What is a person supposed to do with all of these useless ailments? I don't need to suffer anymore. Good-bye, my dear. Call Sonya and tell her that I couldn't wait for her any longer and that I wish her much happiness. Give my clothes and shoes to Lyonya. I think his family will be able to make use of them. Good-bye, my darling. I wish you all the best. Don't think ill of me.
Your Lazar

My dear Sonyechka,
I am sorry for not having written to you for a long time, but in my mind I speak with you every day.

A little time needed to pass before I felt able to sit down and write to you.

After your father's funeral I left for the countryside together with my grandchild, and of course there is never a boring moment when in the company of a four-year-old. I had to pull myself together. Even though I realize that my life is over and that all that is left are the memories, I must go on living. My daughter and my grandson need me. I lived with your father for twenty-two years and we loved each other. Sonyechka, you've asked for pictures. I'm sending you some. He was seldom photographed, only when it was absolutely necessary. The last small picture, a passport photo, was taken because he had to write a request to get a supplement to his pension, but it never came about. He could no longer write.

I'm sending you one of the letters that he wrote to me. He wanted to commit suicide and made an attempt but didn't succeed. I scolded him and said that we have to live our lives with dignity right up to the end. Sonyechka, he suffered so terribly the last year of his life. He grew more and more weak, and of course he knew where it was all heading. The radiation helped alleviate some of the pain, but he suffered from hiccups that could last for weeks at a time. There was no medication for it. Sonyechka, my conscience is clear. I cared for him right up until the very end. I washed him, fed him, and made sure he got the very best of everything.

I've sent all his clothes to Lyonya and given his watch to Denis who was here when he died. Lyalya sent money for the wreath. She couldn't come because her husband was very sick. The minister made a contribution for the funeral. Many people attended. He wasn't forgotten. I have placed the urn in the wall in the lowest row, and now I am planting flowers even though he asked me not to spend time doing that. If you ever manage to get an entry permit, then go the cemetery and pay him a visit.

My dear girl, I am already an old woman. Life has passed so quickly. If only it were possible to predict everything! I would so much like to see you and talk with you. Your father loved you so much. He wanted so badly to live to see you turn forty.

I ask that you don't forget me. I wasn't just his wife, I was also his friend. Write to me. Send me pictures and even better: come visit me. Try going to the embassy and having a talk with them. Maybe I could be allowed to send you an invitation. Then we could go to his grave together, my dear Sonya!

Please be so kind as to remember me. Do you remember the time you came home and caught me in bed with your father? How long ago it all is. And here I am now, sitting and crying, a silly old woman.

I am sending you kisses, my girl, and wish you all the best,
Lara

Transit to Paradise

Tolstoy, fourteen volumes;
Chekhov, seventeen volumes;
Pushkin, six volumes;
Gogol, six volumes;
Dostoevsky, three volumes (of an advance order consisting of twenty-nine volumes);
Lermontov, four volumes;
Bunin, nine volumes;
Turgenev, ten volumes;
Kuprin, six volumes;
Sholom Aleichem, six volumes;
Mark Twain, twelve volumes;

and 117 other books I felt I couldn't live without were placed in a metal chest that had been sent in advance. I was taking the train toward the West and I couldn't imagine life without the Russian classics or Mark Twain's collected works in Russian. In the chest there were also a samovar, a red skirt, and some photographs. I gave away all my clothes and shoes to my girlfriends. I was going to Denmark, to paradise, to the land of milk and honey, where you could have everything. I also had a small metallic icon. I wasn't in the least bit religious, but it was a wedding gift from our close friends and meant a lot to both Ole and me. I had packed it in a small bag made of cloth which I strapped around my waist, concealed under my clothes. It was forbidden to take icons out of the country, but then there was so much that was forbidden.

You couldn't build a Chinese wall around the Soviet Union. Though I'm sure the desire was there! That's why a restricted zone had been established before the actual state border. People should not have the least possible chance of getting anywhere near the border, and it was forbidden even to enter the restricted zone unless you had been given a special permission. If you hadn't, it was impossible to buy an airplane, bus, or train ticket to get there. I had only been in such a zone one time before in my life, but I had never seen a state border.

> The restricted zone was a strip of land along the entire border. In Soviet times it could vary in length from fifty kilometers to half of Kyrgyzstan. Its purpose was to limit the movement of the people. Today Russia's restricted border zone comprises 550,000 square kilometers, but back in the 1970s the Soviet zone was vast: it included the Far East, the entire northern coast along the Polar Ocean, the larger part of Central Asia, including most of southern Kyrgyzstan, South Siberia, and Estonia. Sixteen point four percent of the entire Soviet Union was a restricted zone back then, or, in total, 3,640,000 square kilometers or 84 times the area of Denmark. A very strict inspection of people's documents was conducted upon entering the restricted zone.

My father, my half-sister, and twenty-five of my close friends had come the train station to bid me farewell. I had been giddy with anticipation and mentally had already left. I had said goodbye to my mother in the apartment on Klyuchevaya Street. And I had shut the door, both to the apartment and to the tiny secret room deep within my conscience. Later, there were very few occasions in my life when I dared to open that door again, in spite of the unbearable pain. Behind that door is my mother saying goodbye to me in the year 1970. When we kiss each other goodbye I pretend that I'm just going for a quick trip to Moscow. She does the same. It could very well be a final farewell, but we put on an act in order to ease the parting. I know how horrible it is that I am abandoning her. All mothers know how painful it is when their children move away from home, but in our case it is intensified because she has no idea whether she will ever see me again. That decision is wholly up to the state. The state can permit or forbid visits. Neither of us have any say in the matter. So, in the realm of pain, we kiss each other goodbye and pretend that I will come walking back through that door in a week or so.

The icon was cold to the touch. It was made of brass. Size: 13 by 15 centimeters. Weight: 566 grams. I took it off and placed it next to me when I settled into my compartment and changed into traveling clothes. There was a cacophony of sounds echoing in my mind. I climbed into the upper bunk and fell into the deepest sleep.

I awoke with the Customs officer's face looming over me. The train had stopped at Vyborg, inside the restricted zone. We had to be inspected. All passengers were ordered to exit the compartment. Any nook or corner where a person might be able to hide anything had to be searched. Any place in which things could be concealed. Mattresses would be turned over. But I couldn't just go and leave my icon. I politely asked the officer to step out for a moment so I could put on some clothes. When he left, I once again wrapped the cloth bag containing the icon about my waist so that it was concealed under my dress. In my haste I had not managed to fasten the bag well enough, and I was constantly afraid that I would drop it: crash!

I had to press the icon against my stomach to ensure that it didn't fall out. Touching it relieved the worst of my nervousness. I suddenly had the wherewithal to be daring and convinced the officer that I had been to a going-away party the night before and that everyone had eaten and drunk far too much, myself included. That was why I had a stomachache. And if there is anything that can unite the Russian people, it's a hangover and the results thereof.

Two other officers stepped in and asked whether anybody had anything besides their luggage in the compartment. I immediately showed the receipt for my luggage and followed the first officer out of the train. Outside of every carriage there stood an armed border soldier. Other than that, there wasn't a soul. I felt my stomach as the icon slid down my pubic bone. We hurried to the freight office at the station to examine the contents of my chest.

The officer looked at my library of books, the pictures, and the tea machine I had brought, the samovar. "You can't cure a hangover with tea," he declared philosophically. He looked through my photographs. "What's this?" he suddenly asked as he took up an old photograph of my mother during the War. "You can't take this out of the country." "Keep it," I said. It wasn't exactly the right time to get into a big discussion over that. He put the photo into his pocket and shut the chest. What in the world did he intend to do with my mother's picture?

The receipt for the baggage was stamped. I was told that the chest would be sent off with the next train and arrive in Helsinki the following day. The following day? I started whimpering and explained that I had to get off the train at Helsinki and from there take the boat to Copenhagen a few hours later. The chest *had* to come with me. The officer understood, but there was no one who could lug it up into the train. How in the world was I ever going to get a 100-kilogram chest up in the train? And with an icon that continued to slide further and further down? As did my hand. I was terrified that the train might leave without me. I rushed over to the locomotive with my hands suspiciously close to my private parts. There, the officer's assistant stood smoking a cigarette. He graciously agreed to carry the chest on board together with two border soldiers. It was placed in the baggage compartment. When I returned to the sleeping compartment, the other Customs officers had left. The train could now continue on its way. The books, samovar, and the icon were all taken care of. We could steam full speed ahead through the restricted zone.

We crossed the border during the night. There were bright spotlights. The sight was a blend of a war movie and science fiction. Like the closing credits of a film, several rows of barbed wire floated past the train windows. I was now leaving the Soviet Union together with the Russian, Jewish, and American literary classics as we rode into the darkness of Finland.

The next time I woke up, everything in my mind was silent. As though someone had pressed the mute button and canceled all sound in a film. It was light outside. The landscape that whizzed by outside the windows hadn't changed. They were the same eternally flat stretches populated with pine trees. The train passed by houses and gardens standing freely in the open, but, oddly enough, there were no wooden fences. A red tractor came into view—it was neither black nor brown, which were the usual colors in the Soviet Union, but bright red. I followed it with my eyes until it disappeared into the landscape. I had never before seen a red tractor. It was clear that I was abroad. I was twenty-five years old and had for the first time in my life crossed a state's border. My new passport with my exit permit said Sonya Vesterholt. Shitty Couch remained behind in the Soviet Union.

The train rolled into the main train station of Helsinki. It was the most beautiful place I had ever seen. And there stood my love, Ole, waiting for me on the platform. The world suddenly had colors.

My private "capitalist" was a poor student. And what does a poor student do when he has married the love of his life? He takes a loan at the bank. Ole was determined to buy everything I pointed at on the first day I set foot in the West. I pointed at Tom and Jerry poster outside of a small movie theater at the main train station. I had never seen Tom and Jerry. We bought tickets for the show, and I was completely sold. You couldn't drag me out of the movie theater. I was bid welcome to the capitalist world by two little animals chasing each other for hours on end.

Open, sesame, Ole said, and all the shops in the main train station popped open. Pantyhose and Helena Rubinstein. Marlborough and magic markers. Chewing gum and panties. Aladdin's cave was accessible to everyone. Thankfully for Ole, the other shops were closed that day. It was Sunday.

From the moment I crossed the border I lost the ability of speech and began experiencing the world through pictures. A red tractor. Tom and Jerry. My Russian language remained behind in the Soviet Union, and the only other language I could speak was a tiny bit of French. *Merci* and *comme ci comme ça*. I wouldn't get far with that. When you can't speak with the people around you, you start reading their eyes. I became a deaf-mute, but, on the other hand, my other senses became much more acute.

We boarded the ferry at 10 p.m. The large cold buffet with sumptuous arrangements displayed itself as in the still life paintings of Frans Snyders, which I had seen so often at the State Hermitage Museum in Leningrad. Now this cornucopia of luscious dishes was spread before me on the ferry between Helsinki and Copenhagen. And it was edible!

Ole gave me my first lesson in how to tackle the cold buffet. You start with the herring. We were surrounded by a bunch of noisy children who were hopping and jumping around, and no one said anything or asked them to hush down. In the Soviet Union they would have been stopped a long time ago.

"All happy families resemble one another, but each unhappy family is unhappy in its own way." No, no, I'm not the one who came up with those words. It's the first sentence of Tolstoy's Anna Karenina. According to him, it can't pay to write about happiness. Nothing ever happens. It's boring. And Tolstoy wasn't alone in his conviction. All fairytales end—after the hero has endured numerous trials and tribulations—with the words, "and they lived happily ever after." I had arrived in Denmark. To the end of the fairytale, where I was determined to live happily.

My happiness began in Tåstrup. The chest was placed in the basement. My new family came to visit, and Ole ended up working overtime as full-time interpreter for me. The few bits of French that I knew allowed me to maintain a basic level of conversation. However, when it came to more serious topics, sign language took over. I touched my sister-in-law's beautiful dress and asked nonchalantly, "Mehh?" What I meant to say, of course, was, "Is that beautiful dress made of wool?" My intelligent sister-in-law nodded with understanding and she shook her head. She took my hand and made a crawling movement on it with her fingers mimicking a caterpillar. No, she showed me, it is a silkworm. The dress was made of raw silk. We smiled at each other. For a split second, an understanding had been established. "Mehh," I said again. My life in Denmark had begun.

About the Author

Sonya Vesterholt was born in Tallinn and grew up in Leningrad, all in a country that does not exist now—in the USSR. Then, she married a Danish citizen and moved to Denmark in 1970.

In her first year in Denmark, Sonya worked a conveyer job at Karlsberg's beer factory, and then taught Russian language in the University of Copenhagen for ten years. She opened the first gallery of original posters in Denmark, and then another one. She also studied at the National Danish School of Cinema, from where she graduated in 1989. The same year, she organized Balticum Film & TV Festival, a documentary cinema festival for Baltic countries, in Denmark.

The book *Dog Doing Well* is a result of cooperation, or rather conversations, between Sonya and colleague Britta Sørensen. As many Danish people, Britta initially did not know much about life in the USSR, so Sonya had to add many explanations. The Danish version of this book first appeared in 2011, and by 2017, the fifth edition was underway. These days, new copies are being published regularly, so that the book is always in stock in Danish book shops. The Danish press called the book "a multifaceted little gem with both wisdom and humor and a sense for the individual, and yet so meaningful, detail." One review said: "Two books about the Soviet Union have just been published, an encyclopedia of 600 pages which does not tell much about the difference between our two systems, and a tiny, humorous book of memoirs that says it ALL: *Dog Doing Well* by Sonya Vesterholt."

Dog Doing Well was adapted as a theater play, *Hunden er rask*. CPH Culture has given it the title of the "Best Danish Play" in 2014.

Sonya's next book, *Kærlighedsandet. Fortællinger fra mit liv i Danmark* (The land of love. Stories about my life in Denmark), was published in Denmark in 2016.

In 2017, the book *Dog Doing Well* was translated from Danish into Russian and printed by Sandermoen Publishing in Switzerland.

The author wishes to thank the following persons for their help in preparing the book:
Laura and Peter Bush
Henrik Dal
Ľubomír Ďurovič
Emil Finkelshtein
Aleksandr and Olga Florensky
Susanna Fosgaard Nilsen
Ella Fradkina
Aage and Johanne Louis Hansen Foundation
Rikke Helms
Sten Jakobsen
Jørgen Jørgensen
Ilya Katsnelson
Roni Liebenson
Gita Pasternak
Simon Pasternak
Herbert and Sussi Pundik
Johannes Riis
Mogens Rukov
Betty and Jørgen Sander Laursen
Ilya Utekhin
Velux Fonden Foundation
Tanya Voronina

www.ingramcontent.com/pod-product-compliance
Lightning Source LLC
Jackson TN
JSHW021708150925
91051JS00007B/22